EXTRACT OF THE LIFE OF The AUTHOR

From M. BAYLE.

THAT he was born in *Flanders*, educated at *Paris, Lorrain, Venice, Bologna,* and *Padua*; made great Progress in his Studies, having acquir'd a Knowledge in near Ten different Languages; was sometime in *London*, with the Emperor *Ferdinand*'s Ambassador; returned to *Flanders*, and from thence to *Vienna*, where he was appointed Ambassador to *Solyman the Great*, and soon set out for *Constantinople*; but not finding him there, was obliged to go to *Amasia*, &c. and during his long Stay in that Country, having a strong Propensity to Learning, collected many valuable Manuscripts, Coins, *&c*. Took great Delight in procuring rare Plants, and studying the Nature of Animals; made himself perfect Master of the *Turkish* State, Policy, *&c*. That the Account he composed of his Journey, is a very good Work, and deserves the Approbation of all good Judges; the Learned *Sadelerius*, in his Edition of it, Printed at *Mons*, asserts it deserves a Thousand Impressions. The Celebrated *Thuanus* owns he transcribed many Things out of it to insert in his History, and likewise gives a great Character of the Author and his Work. In short, as we have no good Account of that Country and People, an *English* Version, 'tis presum'd, will be agreeable to the Public.

N. B. *Those who are inclin'd, may see a much larger Account of the Author in* Bayle's *Dictionary,* Vol. II.

SIR,

As I promised you, at parting, to give you a full Account of my Journey to *Constantinople*, so, I shall now make good my Word; and I hope, with Advantage too. For, I shall also acquaint you with my Adventures in my Travel to *Amasia*, as well as That to *Constantinople*, the *former* being less used, and consequently far less known, than the *latter*. My Design herein, is, to allow you a Part of the Solace, of what happened pleasurable to me; for so the ancient Friendship betwixt us obliges me, to appropriate no Joy to myself, without communicating the same to you; but, as for what happened incommodious to me, (as, in so long and tedious a Journey, some Things must needs do) those I take to my self; neither would I have you concerned in them at all; for, the Danger being now past, the more grievous they were to suffer, the more pleasant will they be, even to myself, to remember and commit to Writing.

Upon the Receipt of his Letter, *Ferdinand* was at a stand; he did not fully believe, nor yet altogether disbelieve him; he was inclined to suspect, that the Memory of his *former* Sufferings, and the Fear of *future ones*, did deter him from that Employment, rather than the Danger of his Disease; and yet, on the other side, he did not think it creditable for himself to employ a Man that had so well deserved of him and of the Commonwealth, in any Service against his Will. But the Death of *Malvezius*, which followed a few Months after, did sufficiently convince him, that his Disease was not pretended, to decline the Employment, but was really a Mortal one.

Upon this, I was substituted in the Place of *Malvezius*: But, being unexperienced (as I said before) in the Affairs and Manners of the *Turks*, King *Ferdinand* thought it adviseable for me to bestow a Visit upon *Malvezius* in his Sickness, that so, by his Directions and Advice, I might be better cautioned and armed against any Impositions of the captious *Turks*. Two Days I staid with him, which was as much as the straitness of my Time would permit; and I husbanded them so well, as to be informed by him, what I was to act, and what to avoid, in my daily Convention with the *Turks*.

Whereupon, I posted back to *Vienna*, and began, with great Application and Diligence, to prepare Necessaries for my Journey. But such was the Flush of Business, and so little the Time allowed to dispatch it, that, when the Day fixt for my Departure came, though the King did earnestly press me forward, and I had been extremely Busy all the Day in equipping myself, and in causing Bag and Baggage to be pack'd up, even from the fourth Watch; yet it was the first Watch of the following Night, before I could be quite ready; but then the Gates of *Vienna*, which at that time of Night us'd always to be shut, were opened on purpose for me. The Emperor went abroad a Hunting that Day, but he told his Followers, That he did not doubt but that I would be upon my Way, before he returned from his Sport in the Evening, and it fell out accordingly; yet so, that I was but just gone before he came Home.

At eleven o'Clock at Night, we came to *Ficiminum*, a Town in *Hungary*, four Miles from *Vienna*; there we Supp'd, for our haste was so great that we came Supperless out of Town; from thence we travelled towards *Comora*. The Emperor, among the rest of his Commands, had enjoin'd me to take along with me to *Buda*, one *Paul Palinai* from *Comora*, a Man well acquainted with the Rapins and Depredations of the *Turks*, and so was best able to assist me in my Expostulations with the Bashaw of *Buda*, and in my Demands for satisfaction of Injuries received. But he, not in the least suspecting that my departure would have been so punctual at the Day appointed, had not yet stirred from his own House, and there was no Body could tell when he would come; which uncertainty troubled me very much. I acquainted King *Ferdinand* therewith by Letter, and all the next Day stayed at *Comora* expecting his coming.

But the third Day, I passed over the River *Vaga*, and prosecuted my Journey towards *Gran*, the first Garrison of the *Turks* I came to in *Hungary*. Col. *John Pax*, Governor of *Comora* had sent sixteen Horse with me (of those that the *Hungarians* call *Hussars*) to be my Guard; and he had given them a Charge not to leave me, till they came in sight of the *Turkish* Convoy; for the Governor of *Gran* had signified to me, that his Soldiers should meet me half way. We travelled about three Hours through a vast Plain, when, behold! there appeared afar off four *Turkish* Horse; and yet, notwithstanding, my *Hungarian* Guard accompanied me still, till I desired them to retire; for I was afraid that if they should come up to the *Turks*, some troublesome Bickering would have intervened betwixt them.

As soon as the *Turks* saw me to draw near, they rode up to me, and saluted me by my Coach side: thus we passed on a while together, discoursing interchangeably one with another, (for I had a little Youth for my Interpreter.) I expected no other Convoy, but when we descended into a low Valley, I saw my self on a sudden, surrounded with a Party of about a hundred and fifty Horse. It was a very pleasant Spectacle to a Man, unaccustomed to see such Sights, for their Bucklers and Spears were curiously Painted, their Sword-handles bedeck'd with Jewels, their Plumes of Feathers party-coloured, and the Coverings of their Heads were twisted with round Windings as white as Snow; their Apparel was Purple-coloured, or at least a dark Blue; they rode upon stately Praunsers, adorn'd with most beautiful Trappings. Their Commanders came up to me, and after friendly Salutation they bid me Welcome; and asked me, How I had fared on my Journey? I answer'd them as I thought fit; and thus they led me to *Gran*, for so the Castle is called, situate on an Hill, whose Foot is washed by the *Danow*, with a Town adjoining, built in a Plain. I retired into the Town, the Arch-bishop whereof is Primate of *Hungary*, and for Dignity, Authority and Opulency, is inferior to no Nobleman of that Kingdom.

HERE I was entertained, not after a Courtly, but after a Military manner; for instead of Beds, they spread abroad course shaggy Rugs of Tapestry upon hard Boards; there were no Bed-ticks nor Sheets: Here my Family had the first taste of *Turkish* Delights (forsooth;) as for my self, I fared better, for my Bed was carried along with me wheresoever I went.

THE Day after my Arrival, the *Sanziac* of the Place (for so the *Turks* call a Governor, because a *Sanziac* (*i. e.*) a gilded brass Ball, is carried before him on the top of a Spear, as a Cornet to a Troop of Horse) was very earnest to speak with me; and tho' I had no Letter, nor any other Command to deliver to him, yet such was his importunity, that go I must. And when I came, I found he had no Business with me, but only to see and salute me, and to ask me something of my Errand; and thus, exhorting me to promote a Peace, he wish'd me a happy Journey. In my Passage, I admir'd to hear the croaking of Frogs in such a cold Season of the Year as the Month of *December*; the cause was, the Waters stagnant in those Places are made warm by sulphureous Exhalations.

LEAVING *Gran*, I went towards *Buda*; but to be sure, I took my Breakfast before-hand, which was likely to be my Dinner also; for there was no Place to bait at before I came to *Buda*. The *Sanziac*, or Governor of the Place, with all his Family, together with the Horse which he Commanded, came out of the Town with me, to bring me on my Way: I could by no means persuade him to omit this Office of Respect. The Horse, as soon as they came out of the Gates, began to shew me some sport, curvetting and discharging one against another; they threw their Bonnets on the Ground, and Galloping their Horses with full speed, by them, they took them up by the Points of their Spears; and many such Ludicrous Pranks did they perform. Amongst the rest of them, there was a *Tartar*, who had thick Bushy Hair hanging down over his Shoulders; they told me, that he always went bare Headed, and would never have any other Fence for his Head, either against the Violence of the Weather, or the Hazard of a Battle, but his own Hair. The *Sanziac*, after he had accompanied me as far as he pleased, returned Home, but not before we had taken our Leaves of one another, and he had left some Guides for my Journey, in my Retinue.

When I drew near to *Buda*, a few *Turkish Chiaux*'s met me on the Way, (they are in the Nature of Pursuivants, or Serjeants at Arms, to carry about the Commands of the Grand Seignior, or his Bashaw's, and are Officers of great Esteem in that Nation) by them, I was brought to lodge in the House of a Citizen, who was an *Hungarian*, where my Baggage, Coach and Horses, was better provided for, than myself; for the *Turks* take special Care that Horses, with their Equipage, be well accommodated; as for the Men, if they have but an House over their Heads to shelter them from the Weather, they think they may shift well enough for themselves. The Bashaw of *Buda* sent one to visit me, and bid me welcome, his Name was *Tuigon*, (which in *Turkish*, signifies a Stork) by him he excused himself to me, that he could not admit me into his Presence for some Days, because of a grievous Disease he laboured under; but as soon as ever he recovered a little Strength, he said, he would wait upon me. This Delay was the Occasion, that the aforementioned Absence of *Palinai* was less prejudicial to me, than otherwise it would have been, (to say no more) for he used great Diligence to Post after, lest he might come too late, and accordingly he overtook me a little while after.

I was detained at *Buda* a long Time, by reason of the Sickness of the Bashaw; 'twas thought his Disease was Grief, which he had conceived for the Loss of a great Sum of Money, which was stolen from the Place in which he had hid it, for he was commonly reported to be a Penurious and Sordid-spirited Man. When he heard, that I had brought the Heer *William*

Quacquelben with me, a great Philosopher, and an excellent Physician too, he earnestly intreated me, that he might give him a Visit to administer some Physick to him, in order to his Cure. I easily granted his Request, but soon after, was almost ready to repent of my Facility: For the Bashaw grew worse and worse, and, 'twas thought, he would not have recovered; so that I was afraid, if he had died, the *Turks* would say, my Physician had kill'd him, and by that means, the good Man might have run a great Hazard, and I myself also might have born Part of the Infamy, as being accessary thereunto; but it pleased God to free me from this Anxiety, by restoring the Bashaw to his Health.

'TWAS at *Buda* I got the first Sight of the *Janizaries*, so the *Turks* call the Prætorian Foot; their Number, when it is fullest, is twelve Thousand, and their Prince disperses them all over his Dominions, either to Garrison his Forts against an Enemy, or to be a Safeguard to *Christians* and *Jews*, against the injurious Rage of the Multitude; for there is no well Inhabited Village, Town, or City, wherein there are not some or other of these *Janizarias*, to protect *Christians*, *Jews*, and other helpless Persons, from the Fury of the Rabble. The Castle of *Buda* is always Garrison'd by them; their Habit is a long Garment down to their Ankles, upon their Heads they wear the Sleeve of a Coat, or Cloak (for from thence, as they say, the Pattern was drawn) their Head is put into part of it, and part of it hangs down behind, flapping upon their Shoulders; in the Front, or Fore-part of it, there ariseth a Silver-Cone, somewhat long, gilt over with Gold, and wrought with Jewels, but they were of an ordinary Sort. These *Janizaries* usually came to me by Couples; when they were admitted into my Dining-Room, they bowed down their Heads and made Obeisance, and presently they ran hastily to me, and touched either my Garment, or my Hand, as if they would have kissed it; and then forced upon me a Bundle, or Nosegay of *Hyacinths* or *Narcissus*'s, and presently they retired backward, with equal Speed, to the Door, that so they might not turn their Backs upon me, (for that is accounted undecent, by the Rules of their Order) when they came to the Door, there they stood, with a great deal of Modesty and Silence, with their Hands upon their Breasts, and fixing their Eyes upon the Ground, so that they seemed more like *our* Monks, than *their* Soldiers. But when I had given them some Cash (which was the only Thing they aimed at) they bowed their Heads again, and giving me Thanks with a loud Voice, they wished me all happiness, and departed. The Truth is, unless I had been told before, they were *Janizaries*, I should have thought them to have been a kind of *Turkish* Monks, or Fellows of some College or other amongst them. Yet these are the *Janizaries* that carry such a Terror with them wheresoever they come.

Some *Turks* supp'd with me often at *Buda*, and were mightily taken with the delicious sweetness of my Wine: It is a Liquor that they have but little of in *Turkey*, and therefore, they more greedily desire it, and drink it more profusely, when once they come where it is. They continued Carousing till late at Night, but afterwards I grew weary of the Sport, and therefore rose from Table, and went to my Chamber; but as for Them, they went away sad, because they had not their full Swing at the Goblet, but were able to stand upon their Feet. As soon as I was gone, they sent a Youth after me, desiring me to let them have their Fill of Wine, and that I would lend them my Silver Cups to drink it in; for they were willing, by my Leave, to sit at it all Night in some Corner or other of the House. I granted their Request, and ordered so much Wine to be given them, as they desired, with Bowls to drink it in. Being thus accommodated, they tippled it out so long, till they were even Dead-drunk, and tumbling down, lay fast asleep upon the Ground. You must know, that it is a great Crime in *Turkey* to drink Wine, especially for those who are well stricken in Years; as for the Younger Sort, they think the Offence to be more Venial, and therefore more excusable in them. But seeing they expect no less Punishment, after Death, for drinking a little Wine, than if they drank ever so much, when once they have tasted of that Liquor, they go on to drink more and more; for having once incurr'd the Penalty of their Law, now, they think, they may Sin *gratis*, and account Drunkenness as a Matter of Gain. This Opinion, and others more absurd than This, do the *Turks* hold concerning Wine, of which, I will give you a remarkable Instance: I saw an Old Man at *Constantinople*, who, after he had taken a Cup of Wine in his Hand to Drink, us'd first to make a hideous Noise; I asked his Friends, Why he did so? They answered me, that, by this Outcry, he did, as it were, warn his Soul to retire into some secret Corner of his Body, or else, wholly to Emigrate, and pass out of it, that she might not be guilty of that Sin which he was about to commit, nor be defiled with the Wine that he was to guzzle down.

But to return to *Buda*.

'TWOULD be too tedious for me to give you a large Description of this Place, and it were a Task fitter for one that writes a Book, than a Letter; yet not to be wholly silent, *Buda* lies in a pleasant Place, and in a very fruitful Country, it is extended all along the Brow of an Hill, so that on one Side it borders on a rising Ground, abounding with choice Vineyards, and on the other Side, it is water'd by the River *Danow*, running by it, and beyond the *Danow*, there is the Town of *Pest*, and a large Campain adjoining, both which Prospects are in View of *Buda*, so that this Place seems naturally designed for the Metropolis of *Hungary*. It was antiently adorned with many stately Palaces, belonging to the Nobles of *Hungary*; but those goodly Piles are now either quite fallen to the Ground, or else have many Props to support them from tumbling down; they are Inhabited mostly by the *Turkish* Soldiers, whose daily Pay being but enough to support them, they have no over-plus to lay out in Tyling, or Repairing, such large Structures; and therefore they do not much regard, whether it Rains through the Roof, or whether the Walls be full of Clefts, provided they have a dry Place to set their Horses, and their own Beds in; the upper Part they think concerns them not, so that they make a great Part of the upper Stories to be Inhabited by Weazels and Mice.

BESIDES, 'tis a Piece of Religion in *Turkey*, not to covet magnificent Buildings; for (say they) 'tis a Sign of a Proud, Lofty, and aspiring Mind, to covet Sumptuous Houses, as if so frail a Creature as Man, did promise a kind of Immortality, and an everlasting Habitation to himself in this Life; when alas! we are but Pilgrims here, and therefore, ought to use our Dwellings, as Travellers do their Inns, wherein if they are secured from Thieves, Cold, Heat, and Rain, they seek not for any other Conveniences. So that all over *Turkey* you will hardly find a stately House, tho' the Owner of it be never so Great, or Rich a Man; the Commonalty of them live in Huts and Cottages; the Nobles are for handsome Orchards, Gardens and Baths; but as for their Houses, tho' the numerousness of their Families require large Ones, yet they have no handsome Gate-houses, or Porches belonging to them; nor Court-yards, nor any thing else Magnificent, or worthy of any Admiration. Herein they resemble the *Hungarians*, for except *Buda*, and (perhaps) *Presburgh*, there is scarce any City in *Hungary*, that you can call well Built. This Custom I suppose, they derived from their Ancestors, for they being a People given to Camp-discipline and therein trained, did not care a rush for Building great Houses, but looked upon their Towns only as temporary Habitations, which they were about to leave.

Moreover, whilst I was at *Buda*, I was very much taken with the sight of a strange kind of Fountain that is without the Gate of the Town, in the way leading to *Constantinople*, the Water whereof at top was boiling hot, and yet in the bottom there were Fishes playing up and down; so that you would think, they must needs be throughly boiled, before you could take them out.

'Twas the 7th, of *December*, before the Bashaw was so well recovered as to admit me to his Presence; and then, after I had sweetned him with some Presents, I made my Complaint to him of the Insolency and Ravagings of the *Turkish* Soldiers; and demanded Restitution of what they had wrongfully taken away, contrary to the express of the Truce made, and which he himself, in his Letter to *Ferdinand*, had promised him satisfaction for, if he pleased to send an Envoy to *Buda*. But he, like a cunning Gamester, made as many Complaints of the Injuries and Losses They had sustained by Our Soldiers: And as for his Promise to restore the Places they had wrongfully seized and taken away from the Emperor; he eluded it, by sheltring himself under this Dilemma: *Either I made a Promise, or I did not*; if I made no Promise, then you can demand nothing of me: If I did make a Promise, I know Sir, you are a Person of that Understanding as not to conceive, that I can, or will perform it; for I am sent hither by my Master to Enlarge, not to diminish the Bounds of his Empire; so that I must by no means make his Condition worse than it was: 'tis my Master's Business (Sir) not Mine; what you have to say on this Head, pray propound it to him when you come to *Constantinople*. To be short Sir, you know I am but newly Recovered, and therefore am not in a Condition to maintain any further Discourse. When this course Compliment was put upon me, I thought 'twas time to be gone, neither could I get any thing else from him, only a Truce, till the Grand Seignior's Mind was known.

I observed, that when I was introduced to the Bashaw, they observed the old *Roman* Custom of crying aloud, *Welcome, Welcome*: and so wishing an happy Issue to my Negotiation. I observed also, that the *Turks* count the left Hand to be most Honourable in some particular Cases; the Reason they give is, because the Sword is worn on that side, and he that is on the right Hand has, as it were, the Command of the Sword of him that is at his Left, whereas his Own is free.

MATTERS being thus composed at *Buda*, as well as we could, my Companion *Paliani* returned to the Emperor; but I for my part, shipp'd my Horses, Coaches, and all my Family on some Vessels, prepared for me on the *Danow*, and so passed down the Stream to *Belgrade*; this was a shorter cut, and also more secure; for my Journey by Land to *Belgrade*, would at that Time have cost me at least twelve Days, especially, having such a deal of heavy Baggage with me; and besides, we had been in danger to be Robb'd by the *Heyduc*'s, so the *Hungarians* call a sort of plundering Thieves and Robbers; but upon the Water there was no fear at all of them; and besides, we compassed our Journey in five Days. The Vessel in which I was, was drawn along by a lesser Pinnace, in which there were twenty-four Oars; the other Vessels had but two large Oars a-piece. The Mariners rowed Night and Day without any Intermission, excepting only a few Hours that the poor Souls borrow'd to Sleep and Eat in. In my Passage down the River, I could not but observe the venturousness, not to say temerity of the *Turks*, who were not afraid to Sail on in the mistiest Weather and darkest Night, and when the Wind blew very hard too; and besides, there were many Water-mills, with several Trunks and Boughs of Trees hanging over the Banks, which made our Passage very Dangerous; so that some times our Vessel, by the boisterousness of the Wind, was driven to the Bank, and there dash'd against old stumps of Trees hanging over, so that it was like to split; this is certain, that she lost some Planks out of her Hulk, which made a terrible crack and noise when they were loosed therefrom. This noise awak'd me; leaping out of my Bed, I advis'd the Mariners to be more cautious: they lift up their Voices, and gave me no other Answer than *Alaure*, i. e. *God will help*, and so I might go to Bed again, if I would.

THO' we speed pretty well, yet I am apt to believe, that at one Time or other, such Dangerous Sailing will be fatal to some Passengers. In our Passage, I saw *Tolna*, a handsome Town in *Hungary*; I cannot forbear to mention it, because there we had very good White-wine, and, besides the Inhabitants were very Courteous to us. Moreover, we passed in sight of the Castle of *Walpot*, seated on an Hill, and of other Castles and Towns besides; we saw also, where the River *Drave*, on the one side, and the *Tibiscus*, or *Taise*, on the other, made their Influx into the *Danow*. As for *Belgrade* itself, it is seated at the confluence of the *Save* and the *Danow*; the old City is built in the extreme Angel of the Promontory, the Building is old, it is fortified with many Towers, and a double Wall: Two parts of it are wash'd by the *Save*, and the *Danow*, but on that part where it is joined to the Land, it hath a very strong Castle on high Ground, consisting of many loftly Turrets made of square Stone; before you come into the City, there is a vast Number of Buildings, and very large Suburbs, wherein several Nations inhabit, *viz. Turks, Greeks, Jews, Hungarians, Dalmatians,* and many others. For you must know that ordinarily over all the *Turkish* Dominions, the Suburbs are larger than the Towns, but take them both together, they give the resemblance of large Cities: 'Twas at this Town, that I first met with some ancient Coins, wherein, as you know, I take a great delight, and my Physician aforesaid, Dr. *Quackquelben,* fitted me to an Hair, as we say, for he was as much addicted to those Studies as myself. I found a great many Pieces, which on one side represented a *Roman* Soldier, placed between a Bull and a Horse, (for 'tis known, that the Legions of upper *Mæsia* did anciently encamp hereabouts) with this Inscription, *Taurunum.* This City, in the memory of our Grandfathers, was twice violently assaulted by the *Turks,* first, under *Almurath*; next under *Mahomet,* who took *Constantinople*; but the *Hungarians,* under the Banner of the Cross, made such a vigorous Defence, that the *Barbarians* were beaten off with a great deal of Loss. But at last, in the Year 1520. *Solomon,* in the beginning of his Reign, came before it with a vast Army, and finding it, either by the neglect of young King *Ludovicus,* or by the Discords of the factious *Hungarian* Nobles, destitute of a Garrison able to defend it, he took that opportunity to assault it, and so easily became Master thereof. And that Door being once opened, an *Iliad* of Miseries broke in upon poor *Hungary,* of which she is sadly Sensible to this Day; for this Pass being gained, there followed the Slaughter of King *Lewis Ludovicus,* the taking of *Buda,* the inslaving of *Transilvania,* and a flourishing Kingdom, hereby brought under the Yoke, not without a Terror struck into the Neighbouring Nations, least they also should partake of the same Calamities; by which Example, Christian Princes may take warning, never to think their Frontier Towns and Castles to be strong enough, nor sufficiently provided against so potent an Enemy as the *Turk.* For the Truth is, the *Ottomans* are herein not unlike to great Rivers, whose Swelling Waves, if they break down any part of the Bank or Jitty, that keeps them in, spread far and near, and do abundance of Mischief; so the *Turks,* but far more perniciously, having once broke through the Obstacles that stopt them, make a vast spoil where-ever they come. But to return to *Belgrade*, that I may prosecute the rest of my Journey to *Constantinople*.

AFTER I had provided myself in that City of all Things necessary for a Land Journey, I left *Semandria*, heretofore a Town or Castle, of the despots of *Servia*, on the left side of the *Danow*; from whence we Journied towards *Nissa*. In our way thither, the *Turks* shewed us, from the higher Grounds, the Mountains of *Transilvania*, with Snowey Tops, but at a great Distance from us, and moreover, they pointed with their Fingers, were the Ruins of *Trajans* Bridge were: After we had past the River called *Morava*, we came to a Town of the *Servians*, named *Jagodna*; there I observed the Funeral Rites of that Country, which differ very much from ours, as you may find by this Relation following.

THE dead Body was placed in a Temple, with the Face uncovered; near it were laid Victuals, as Bread, Flesh, and a Flagon of Wine: The Wife and Daughter of the Deceased stood by, in their best Apparel; the Daughter's Hat was made of Peacocks Feathers. The last Boon that the Wife bestowed on her dead Husband, was a Purple Bonnet, such as noble Virgins us'd to wear in that Country. Then we heard their Funeral Plaints, Mourning and Lamentations, wherein, they asked the dead Corps, How they came to deserve so ill at his Hands? Wherein had they been wanting in their Duty and Observance, that he had left them in such a lonesome and disconsolate Condition? And such like Stuff. The Priests that ministred in this Service, were of the *Greek* Church. In the Church-Yard, there were erected on Poles, or long Staves, several Pictures of Stags, Hinds, and such Kind of Creatures, cut in Wood; when I asked them the Reason of this strange Custom, they told us, That their Husbands, or Fathers, did thereby signify the Celerity and Diligence of their Wives or Daughters, in managing their Houshold Affairs. Moreover, by some Sepulchres, there hung Bushes of Hair, which Women, or Maidens, had placed in Testimony of their Grief for the Loss of their Relations. We were also informed, that it was the Custom of that Country, after Friends on both Sides had accorded about the Marriage of a young Couple, for the Bridegroom to snatch away his Bride, as it were by Force; for they do not think it handsome, that a Maid should consent to her own Devirgination, or first Nights Lodging with her Husband.

AT a small Distance from *Jagodna*, we met with a little River which the Neighbouring Inhabitants called *Nissus*, and we kept it on our right Hand almost all the Way till we came to *Nissa*; yea, and beyond the Town, upon the Bank thereof (were there were some Remains of an old *Roman* Way) we saw a small Marble Pillar, yet standing, wherein there were some *Latin* Letters inscribed; but they were so defaced, that they could not be read: As for the Town of *Nissa*, for that Country, it is a decent one, and full of Inhabitants.

'TIS Time now to acquaint you with the Entertainment we met with at our Inns, for I believe you long to know. When I came to *Nissa*, I lodged in a public Inn; the *Turks* call them *Caravarsarai*, of which there are a great many in that Country; the Form of them is thus, it is a large Edifice, that has more of Length than Breadth; in the midst of it, there is a kind of Yard for the placing of Carriages, Camels, Mules and Waggons. This Yard is compassed about with a Wall about three Foot high, which joins, and is, as it were, built in the outward Wall that incloses the whole Building; the Top of this inner Wall is plain and level, and is about four Foot broad. Here the *Turks* lodge, here they sup, and here is all the Kitchen which they have (for in the ambient Wall before spoken of, there are ever and anon some Hearths built) and here are no Partitions between Camels, Horses, with other Cattel, and Men, but the Space of that inner Wall; and yet at the Foot of that Wall, they so tye their Horses, that their Heads and Necks are above it, or at least may lean over it; and thus, when their Masters are warming themselves at the Fire, or else are at Supper, they stand near them as Servants us'd to do; and sometimes they will take a Piece of Bread or Apple, or whatsoever else is offered them, out of their Masters Hand. Upon the same Wall, the *Turks* make their Beds, after this Manner, first of all they spread a broad Piece of Tapestry, which is fitted as a Saddle-cloth by Day, for their Horses; upon that they put their Cloaks, their Saddles serve for a Pillow, and with the long Vests they wear at Day, they cover themselves at Night. And thus they take their rest, never provoking Sleep by any other Allurement. There is nothing done in secret, there all is open, and every Body may see what another does, unless the Darkness of the Night hinder him. For my Part, I greatly abhored this Sort of Lodging, because the Eyes of all the *Turks* were continually upon us, staring and wondering at our Carriage, according to the Customs of our Country. And therefore, I always endeavoured to lodge at the mean House of some poor Christian! but alas! their Cottages were so small, that many Times I had not room enough in them for placing my Bed; so that sometimes I slept in my Tent, sometimes in my Coach, and sometimes again I turned into the *Turkish* Hospitals; which, to give them their due, are very convenient, and not unhandsomely built, for they have several distinct Apartments for Lodgings in them. There is no Man forbid the Use of them, either *Christian* or *Jew*, Rich or Poor, they are open equally to all. Even the *Bashaw*'s and *Sanziacs*, when they travel, make use of them. In these I thought myself lodg'd as well as in the Palace of a Prince.

THE Custom of these Inns, like Hospitals, is this: They allow Victuals to every particular Man, that comes in as a Guest: So that when Supper-time came, there was a Servant that brought in a great wooden Dish almost as big as a Table; in the middle of it was a Platter full of Barley boiled to a Jelley, with a little Piece of Flesh, and about the Platter were some small Loaves, and here and there a Piece of an Honey-comb. When I saw this, at first, out of Modesty, I refused it, saying, that my Servants were preparing my own Supper for me, and therefore, advised them to give it to the Poor: He took it amiss, and prest it upon me, and alledging, that I should not scorn their slender Provision, that the Bashaw's themselves us'd to eat it; it was the Custom of their Country so to do; they had enough left to give to the Poor, and if I would not eat it my self, I should give it my Servants; hereupon, I was enforced to take it, that I might not be counted uncivil by them; and after I had tasted a little of it, I gave him Thanks. The Relish of it pleased me well, for that kind of Gruel, as it is commended by *Galen*, so it is very wholesome, and not unpleasing to the Taste. Travellers may be entertained with that kind of Diet for three Days; but when that Time is expired, they must pack up and be gone. Here (as I told you) I was well entertained; but I met not always with such good Quarters. Sometimes, when I could not light upon an House, I lodged in a Stable; my People enquired after a large and capacious one, in one part whereof was an Hearth and a Chimney, and the other part was design'd for the Herds of Cattle; for that is the Make of the *Turkish* Stables, that the Herd and the Herdsman lodge under the same Roof. I divided that part where the Fire was from the rest, by the sides of my Tent, and then I put my Table and my Bed by the Fire-side, and liv'd like an Emperor: As for my Family, they wallowed in a great deal of clean Straw, in the other part of the Stable: But some of them fell a Sleep by the Fire-side in the adjoining Orchard or Meadow where a

Supper was preparing; the heat of the Fire was their guard against the coldness of the Night, and they had as great a care not to let it go out, as the *Vestal Virgins* had of old at *Rome*.

I suppose, you will ask me, how my Family relieved themselves against the inconvenience of their bad Lodging; especially seeing they could have little Wine in the middle of *Turkey*, which might have been some Remedy for their ill Lodging at Night. For the truth is, there is little Wine to be had in several of their Villages, especially, if no *Christians* dwell among them: For I must tell you, that the *Christians* being wearied out with the Pride and Insolency of the *Turks*, do many times withdraw themselves from the common Road into desert Places; which tho' they are less fruitful, yet are more secure; and so leave their better Possessions to the domineering *Turks*. And whenever we drew near to any such Places, where there was no Wine, the *Turks* would very fairly tell us of it before-hand; so that I sent my Steward the Day before, with a *Turk* to guide him, to procure some from the next Villages of the *Christians*. And by this means it was, that the Distresses of my Family were something alleviated; 'tis true, I could not get any soft Feather-beds or Pillows for them, or other Blandishments for Sleep; the Wine was instead of all: As for myself, I had some Flagons of choice Wine in my Chariot, so that I wanted none; thus I and my Family were provided for, as to Wine.

But, there was one Inconvenience, which troubled us more than the Scarcity of Wine, and that was, our Sleep was miserably interrupted; for we being to rise betimes in the Morning, and sometimes before Day, that we might come the sooner to our Inns at Night; our *Turkish* Guides being deceived by the Light of the Moon, would sometimes call us up at, or about Midnight, with a great deal of Noise and Clamour. For the *Turks* have no Clocks to distinguish Hours, nor Miles to shew the Distance of Places: Only they have a sort of Ecclesiasticks, which they call *Talismans*; this sort of People use a kind of Admeasurement by Water, and when they perceive thereby, that 'tis Morning, then they cry aloud from an high Tower, built on purpose, exhorting them to arise and worship God. They make the same Noise in the middle between Sun-rise and Noon, and likewise, between Noon and Sun-set; and, last of all, when the Sun is set, they cry out with a very shrill Voice, which hath no unpleasant Modulation, and which is heard farther than any Body would think. Thus the *Turks* divide the Day into four

Spaces, longer or shorter, according to the Season of the Year: But for the Night-time, they have no certain Rule at all.

So our *Turkish* Guides being deceived by the exceeding Brightness of the Night they called us up before Sun-rising, and we started out of our Beds in great Haste, that so they might not impute any unlucky Accident, upon the Way, to our Slothfulness; in the Morning, we pack'd up our Baggage, and put my Bed and Tent in our Waggons, harnessed our Horses, and were ready for our Journey, only expected the Word of Command. But our *Turks*, when they found their Mistake, fairly went into their Nests again, and after we had waited for them a great while, I sent to them, to tell them, we were all ready; and now the Delay was on *their* Side, my Messengers brought me Word, from them, that the Moon-light had deceived them, and therefore, they were gone to sleep again, for it would be a great while before it would be Time to go; and they persuaded us to try to sleep again too. And thus, we must either unpack all our Things again, to our no small Trouble, or else, we must endure a great Part of the Coldness of the Night in the open Air.

To prevent this Inconvenience for the future, I charged the *Turks* not to be so troublesome any more, as to rouze me out of my Sleep, for if they would but tell me over Night, at what Time they would rise in the Morning, I would be sure to be ready at the Time appointed; for I had Watches by me, that I intended to make Use of, which would not fail to acquaint me with the precise Hour of the Morning; and if they over-slept themselves, they should lay it to my Charge, so that they need not scruple to trust me with the Hour of their rising. They seemed to be somewhat satisfied herewith, and yet did not lay aside all their Solicitude neither; for in the Morning betimes, they awakened my *Valet de Chambre*, desiring him to go to me, and to see how the Index of my Watches did pointed; he so, and returned Answer to them, as well as he could, That 'twas very near Sun-rising, according as he found it. When they had thus tried him once or twice, and found that he hit the Time right, they trusted me for the future, and admired the Structure of our Watches, that could so faithfully declare the Time; so that ever after, we slept out our Sleep, without any Disturbances from them.

From *Nissa* we came to *S. Sophia*; the Journey thither, and the Weather, for that Time of the Year, was very tolerable. *Sophia* is a Town big enough, and well inhabited both by Citizens and Strangers: It was heretofore the Royal Seat of the King of *Bulgaria*; and afterwards, if I mistake not, of the

Despots of *Servia*, whilst that House stood, before it was overthrown by the *Turkish* Arms.

Afterwards, we continued our Journey, for many Days, through the pleasant, and not unfruitful, Valley of *Bulgaria*; all the Time we were in that Country, we had little other Bread, but only Cakes bak'd under Ashes upon the Hearth, which they call *Togatch*. The Women and Maids sell them, for they have no Bakers in those Parts; and when they perceive any Guests a-coming, that are likely to pay for what they have, presently they knead a little Dough, with Water, without any Leaven, and lay it upon Tiles, under the Ashes, and so bring it out piping hot, and sell them for a very small Matter; other Victuals is also very cheap there, a good Weather-sheep may be bought for thirty-five Aspers; a Chicken and a Hen for an Asper, a sort of Coin with them, of which fifty make but a Crown.

I must not omit to acquaint you with the Habit of these *Bulgarian* Women. They commonly wear nothing but a Smock or Shift, made of no finer Linnen-thread, than that we make Sacks of. And yet, these course Garments are wrought by them, with several sorts of strip'd Needle-work, after a homely Fashion: With this lose party-coloured Habit they mightily pleased themselves, so that when they saw our Shifts, made of the finest Linnen, yet they wondered at our Modesty, that we could be contented to wear them without various Works of divers Colours wrought in them.

But that which I most of all admired in them, was the Tower, which they wore on their Heads, for such was the Form of their Hats. They were made of Straw, braided with Webs over them. The Figure of them differs from the Hats Women wear in our Country, for ours hang down on the Shoulders, and the lowest Part of it is the broadest, and so it rises as it were into a Pyramid at top; but theirs is narrowest below, and so rises up like a top, almost nine Inches above the Head; but that Part of it that looks upwards, towards the Sky, is both very capacious, and also very open, so that it seems made to take in Rain, as ours are to shelter us against them; but in that Space, interjacent between their upper and lower Part, their hang Pieces of Coin, little Pictures or Images, small Parcels of painted Glass, or whatever is resplendent, though never so mean, which are accounted very ornamental among them.

Those kind of Hats makes them look taller, and also more Matron-like, though they are easily blown off their Heads, by a blast of Wind, or by any light Motion they fall off themselves.

When they appeared to us in this Dress, I thought they resembled *Clytemnestra*, or some *Hecuba* or other, in the flourishing Time of *Troy*, coming upon the Stage. This Sight suggested to me some pious Meditations, *viz.* How frail and mutable a Thing that which is called *Nobleness of Birth, is*; for when I asked of some of these Lasses, they that seemed to be the handsomest among them, concerning their Stock and Lineage, they told me, They were descended from the Chief Nobles of that Country; and some of them were of a Royal Progeny, though now it was their Fate, to marry Herdsmen or Shepherds: For Nobility is very little esteemed in the *Turkish* Dominions. For, I my self did afterwards see at *Constantinople*, and other Places, some Descendants from the Imperial Families of the *Catacuzeni*, and the *Palæologi*, living more contemptuously among the *Turks*, than ever *Dionysius* did of old at *Corinth*; nay, the *Turks* esteem no Men for their Birth, but only for their own perform'd Accomplishments, excepting only the *Ottoman Family*; for that they have a high Veneration, upon Account of its Original.

It is thought that these *Bulgarians* had their Original from *Seythia*, near the River *Volga*, and that they changed their Habitations and came into these Parts, when other Nations, either compelled by Force, or prompted by Choice, changed theirs; and that they were called *Bulgarians*, i. e. *Volgarians*, from the River *Volga*, aforesaid. Upon this Transmigration, they fix'd their Habitation upon those Parts of Mount *Hæmus*, that lie between *Sophia* and *Philippopolis*, which are Places naturally strong; where they, for a long Time, baffled all the Power of the *Grecian* Emperors, and killed *Baldwin* the Elder, Earl of *Flanders*, then Emperor of *Constantinople*, after they had taken him in an hot Skirmish. Yet, for all this, they were not able to resist the Power of the *Turks*, but were overcome and miserably enslaved by them. They use the *Illyrian*, or *Slavonian* Tongue, as the *Servians* and *Rascians* also do.

Before a Man descends into that Plain that lies over against *Philippopolis*, he must go through a Forest and a craggy Mountain, which the *Turks* call *Carpi Dervent*, i. e. *The Gate of the strait or narrow Passage*; but in the Plain before-mentioned, we met with the River *Hebrus*, having its

Original from the adjoining Mountain *Rhodope*. Before we could pass the said Straits, we saw the Top of Mount *Rhodope* all cover'd over with deep Snow. The Inhabitants, as I remember, call it *Rulla*. From hence flows the River *Hebrus*, as *Pliny* says, and *Ovid* also affirms the same in this Distick.

Qua patet umbrosum Rhodope glacialis ad Hæmum,
Et sacer amissas exigit Hebrus aquas.

> *Where Icy* Rhodope *ope's to shady* Hœme,
> *And sacred* Hebrus *wants part of her Stream.*

IN which Verses, the Poet seems to intimate the Shallowness of that River for want of Water. For though it is a great and famous River, yet, in most Places it is fordable: For, I remember, in my return from *Constantinople*, we forded over it near *Philippopolis*, to an Island on the other Side, where we lay in Tents all Night; but it happened, that the Waters swelled that Night by reason of Rain, that next Morning we could not repass the River, to come into the Road, without a great deal of Trouble.

THE City of *Philippopolis* is situate on one of the three little Hills, disjoyned, and, as it were, rent from the rest of the Mountains, and is, as the Grace of those little Hillocks. While we were at *Philippopolis*, we saw Rice growing like Wheat, in the watry and marshy Grounds. The whole Plain, about the Town, is full of little round Hills of Earth, which the *Turks* say, were raised on Purpose, as Monuments of the frequent Battles fought in those Fields, and the Graves such as were slain there. From hence, leaving the River *Hebrus* something on the Right, and Mount *Hæmus*, which runs forth into *Pontus*, on the left, at last we passed over the *Hebrus* on a famous Bridge, made by *Mustapha*, and so came to *Hadrianople*, which the *Turks* call *Endrene*.

THIS City was formerly called *Orestia*, before the Emperor *Hadrian* inlarged it, and called it by his own Name. It is seated at the confluence of the River *Mariza* or *Hebrus*, and the two small Currents of *Thinsa* and *Harda*, which there meeting in a joint Stream run into the *Egean Sea*. This City is not very large within the Walls; but, if you take in the Suburbs, and the Buildings which the *Turks* have added without, it is very capacious.

WE staid but one Day at *Hadrianople*, and then went forward on the last Stage of our Journey towards *Constantinople*. In my Way thither there grew abundance of *Narcissus's Hyacinth's*, and (as the *Turks* call them) *Tulips*, which we beheld, not without Admiration, that in the midst of Winter, which is not favourable to such Flowers in other Countries, the Ground should be so garnished by them. As for *Narcissus's*, and *Hyacinths*, all

Greece abound with them; and they are so odoriferous, that, by reason of their Multitude, they are offensive to those Heads that are unaccustomed to such Kind of Smells. But the *Tulip*, hath little or no Smell, but its gaudiness and party-colouredness is its greatest Commendation. The *Turks* are great Admirers of Flowers, so that, though they are Parsimonious enough in other Cases, yet for a stately Flower, they will not scruple to give some *Aspers*. And the Truth is, these kind of Flowers, though they were presented to me as a Gift, yet they cost me a great deal of Money; for some *Aspers* were always expelled in requital. Neither is there any other way of treating with a *Turk*, but by opening the Purse-strings, as soon as any *Christian* comes among them; neither must he think to shut them again, till he go out of their Country: While he is there, he must scatter his Coin, and if he get no other Advantage by it, yet it makes them more tractable. For the *Turks* are so ill-natured, and such under-valuers of all Nations but their own, that without this Open-handedness, there were no more living among them, for Strangers, than in the most desolate and uninhabited Places, by reason of the excessiveness either of Cold or Heat; but with the Bait of Liberality, you may catch a *Turk* at any Time.

About the mid-way between *Hadrianople* and *Constantinople*, there is a little Town, called *Chiurli*, memorable for the *Overthrow* which *Selimus* received in a Battle against his Father *Bajazet*, out of which he escaped by the Swiftness of his Horse, called *Carabonluch*, i. e. a *Black Cloud*, and so fled to the *Cham*, or the *Precopeian Tartar*, who was his Father-in-Law.

Before we came to *Selimbria*, which is a Town standing on the Sea-side in our Way, we saw the Ruins of an old Wall and Ditch, which were made by the later Emperors of *Greece*, which reached from that Sea to the *Danow*, to secure all that was contained within that Fortification to the *Constantinopolitans*, against the Incursions of the *Barbarians*; and there goes a Story, that when that Wall was a Building, a certain old Man delivered his Opinion to his Wife, *viz*. That that Wall would not so much secure what was within it, from the Hands of the Infidels, as it would expose and subject it to their Rage and Fury, in regard it would add Courage to the *Barbarians* to assault it, and weaken the Courage of the *Grecians* to defend it.

At *Selimbria* we had a most pleasant Prospect of a calm Sea; and 'twas very pleasant to us to behold the smooth Water, and to gather Cockles on the Shore; yea, to behold Sholes of *Dolphins* sporting in the Water, which, with the Warmness of the Air, was exceeding delightful. It can hardly be imagined, how mild the Weather was in those Parts, though sometimes it be a little more boisterous at *Chiurli*; but here there is, as I may call it, a *Thracian Gale*, and an incredible Sweetness of Air.

WHEN we came near to *Constantinople*, we passed over two pleasant Arms of the Sea, upon a Bridge built over them. I may safely say, That if those Places were cultivated by Art, as they are naturally pleasant, the Sun never shone on a better Country; but, alas! they seem to mourn for the Neglect put upon them by the insulting *Barbarian*. Here we had our Fill of choice Sea-fishes, which were even taken in our Sight.

WHEN I lodged in those Inns the *Turks* call *Imaret*, I usually observed, that the Cracks of the Walls were all full of Pieces of Paper; and thinking something was the Matter, but not knowing what, I took out some of them, and finding nothing writ therein of any Consequence, I was more earnest to know of the *Turks* the Reason of their so doing; especially as I had observed the same Thing in other Places of *Turkey* before. At first they scrupled to tell me, as thinking perhaps that I would not believe them; or else, not being willing to impart so great a Mystery of Things to such an Alien as myself. This made me the more inquisitive, till at last some of them, with whom I became more familiar, told me, That the *Turks* gave a great deal of Difference to Paper, because the Name of God may be written in it: And, therefore, they will not suffer the least Bit of Paper to lie upon the Ground, but presently they take it up, and thrust it into some Chink or Hole or other, that so it may not be trampled under Foot; and hitherto, perhaps, their Superstition may be tollerable, but mark what follows.

IN the Day of Judgment, say they, when *Mahomet* shall call up his Followers from their *Purgatory*, (to which they were condemned for their Sins) to Heaven, to be there made Partakers of Eternal Blessedness; there will no Way be left for them to come to their Prophet, but over an huge red-hot Iron Grate, which they must run over bare-foot, (how painfully, you may guess, when you imagine a Cock to skip thro' hot-burning Coals.) But at that Instant, (believe it if you can!) all those Bundles of Papers, which they have preserved from being trod upon, will immediately appear, and put themselves under their Feet; by which Means they will pass the red-hot Iron-Grate with less Damage; so necessary do they count the Work of saving a little Paper. And, to add to the Story, I remember that my *Turkish* Guides were once very angry with my Servants, for making use of Paper to cleanse their *Posteriors*, and thereupon made a grievous Complaint to me of their horrid Offence therein: I had no Way to put them off, but by telling them, 'twas no Wonder my Servants did such strange Things, seeing they also used to eat Swines Flesh, which the *Turks* abhor. Thus I have given you a Taste of the *Turkish* Superstition; I shall add, That they account it a damnable Sin, if any of their own People chance (though unwillingly) to sit upon the *Alcoran*, (which is a Book containing the Rites of their Religion) and, if a *Christian* do it, 'tis Death by their Law. Moreover, they will not suffer *Rose-Leaves* to lie upon the Ground, because, as the Ancients did fable, the Roses spring out of the Blood of *Venus*; so the *Turks* hold, That it had its Rise from the Sweat of *Mahomet*.

I came to *Constantinople* on the 20th Day of *January,* and there found my Collegues above-mentioned, *Anthony Wrantzius* and *Francis Zay*; as for the *Grand Seignior* himself, he was, at that Time, at the Head of his Army in *Asia*, and had only left at *Constantinople, Ebrahim Bashaw,* an Eunuch, as Governor of the City, and *Rustan,* but deprived of his Vizier-ship; however I gave him a Visit and made him Presents, as being mindful of his former Dignity, and of the fair Prospect there was of his speedy Restitution thereunto.

IT may, perhaps, divert you, and besides it is not wholly foreign to my Design, to acquaint you how this *Rustan* came to be strip'd of all his former Honours. Know then, That *Solyman* had a Son, called *Mustapha,* on a Concubine of his, born by the *Bosphorus,* (if I mistake not.) This Youth was in the prime of his Age, and in great Favour among the Soldiers. But the same *Solyman* had several other Children by *Roxolana,* whom he doated on so much, that he made her his Wife, by appointing her a Dowry; for that's the Way of making and confirming a Marriage among the *Turks*. This *Solyman* did, contrary to the Custom of former Emperors, none of which had ever married a Wife, since the Days of *Bajazet* the Elder; the Reason was, because the said *Bajazet,* being overthrown by *Tamerlane,* was, with his Wife, taken Prisoner by him, where he suffered many Indignities, but none affected him more, than the Uncivilities and Reproaches which he saw offered to his *Sultaness,* before his Face. The Memory of which Affronts made such a deep Impression on all those that succeeded *Bajazet* in the

Empire, that, to this very Day, none of them will marry a Wife, that so, whatever Chance should happen, they might never fall into the like Indignity; so that, ever since, they beget Children on Women of a servile Condition, in whose Misfortunes they may be less concerned, than if they were their lawful Wives. And yet the Children begot on such Concubines, are as much esteemed by the *Turks*, as if they were born in lawful Wedlock, and they have as much right to their Fathers Estates.

So then, *Mustapha*, being of a promising Ingenuity, and in the Flower of his Age; and besides, being the Darling of the Soldiers, and the common People too, having so many favourable Circumstances attending him, he, after his Father's Death, was by the Votes of all designed for his Successor in the Empire.

On the other Side, his Stepmother, *Roxalana*, with Might and Main, laboured to prevent it, and to secure the Empire for the Children begotten on her own Body, and thereupon presuming on her Marriage-Relation, she ceased not to disparage *Mustapha*, and to prefer a younger Son of her own before him. In this Design *Rustan* was both her Counsellor, and Assistant; they drew both in one Yoke, for *Rustan* having married a Daughter of *Solyman*'s, by *Roxalana*, their Interests thereupon were reciprocal.

This *Rustan* was the Chief of the Bashaw's, and *Solyman*'s Prime Vizier, having the chief Power and Authority with him: He was a Man of a sharp and very capacious Wit, and a great Grace to *Solyman*'s Government. As for his Original, he was the Son but of a Shepherd, and yet he seemed worthy of that Dignity to which he was advanced, if his sordid Avarice had not been a Blot in his Escutcheon. And to speak truly, *Solyman* himself observed this Vice in him, though upon all other Accounts, he was his choice and only Favourite: And yet this Crime of his turned to his Master's Advantage; for being appointed by *Solyman* to preside over his Treasury, or Exchequer, which sometimes was very low, he was so thrifty in the Management of that Office, that he did not spare to raise Money, even by the meanest and most contemptible Ways. For he laid a Tax on Herbs, Roses, and Violets, which grew in great Men's Gardens; he caused the Armour, Coats of Mail, Warrior's Horses, of such as were taken Prisoners in War, to be sold, and by such Ways as those he got together such a Mass of Money, that *Solyman* was very secure on that Part; upon this Occasion, I remember, that a great Man among the *Turks*, who are usually vindictive enough, that was a great Enemy to *Rustan*, yet (to my Surprize) told me, That he would do *Rustan* no hurt, tho' it were never so much in his Power, because his Care and Industry had advanced his Master's Treasury to so prodigious a Sum. There is a Chamber in the *Seraglio*, at *Constantinople*, over which there is this Inscription, *Here is the Cash obtained by the Diligence of* Rustan.

When *Rustan* was Grand Vizier, and had the intire Administration of all Things in his Hands, he was able to turn his Master's Mind, as he pleased, so that 'twas commonly reported among the *Turks*, That partly by the Accusation of *Rustan*, and partly by the Witchcraft of his Wife *Roxolana*, (for she was accounted little better than a Sorceress) *Solyman* was so alienated from his Son *Mustapha*, that he took Counsel to put him to Death. As to what some alledge, that *Mustapha* being sensible of the Designs of *Rustan* and his Step-Mother *Roxolana*, against his Life, did labour to preserve them, by taking off his Father, and so seizing the Empire by force; very few do believe that Story, but look upon it as a Fiction.

On this Occasion, let me tell you, that the Sons of the *Turkish* Emperors are the miserablest Creatures in the World; for if any one of them succeed his father in the Empire, the rest are inevitably put to Death by him. For the *Turks* cannot endure any Corrival in Government; and besides they are egged on to this severity by their *Prætorian* Bands, (*Janizaries* and *Spahies*) who, as long as there is any one of the *Grand Seigniors* Brothers alive, never cease craving of Largesses and Boons, and if the present Emperor refuses to grant them, they presently cry out, *God save your Brother, God send your Brother a long Life*; by which Words, they more than intimate their Wishes, that he were on the Throne. So that the *Turkish* Emperors are in a manner compelled to put their Brethren to Death, and so begin their Reign with Blood. But *Mustapha* was afraid of such a fatal end; or else *Roxolana* was willing to translate the said Destiny from her own Children upon *Mustapha*: Upon one or other of these Grounds, it was, that *Solymon* entertain'd the thought of putting his Son *Mustapha* to Death. And the occasion fell out opportunely, for he had War at that Time, with *Sagthama* King of the *Persians*, thither *Rustan* was sent with a vast Army. When he drew near to the Borders of *Persia*, upon a sudden he made a stop, and wrote back fearful Missives to *Solyman*, telling him, *That the whole Empire was in great hazard, there was nothing but Treason studied in the*

Army, they all cry'd out A Mustapha! A Mustapha! *yea, the Disease was grown to such a height, that 'twas past his skill to cure it; and therefore the Emperor himself must come immediately, if he would have the Crown sit safe on his Head.*

SOLYMAN was mightily disturb'd at the News, and therefore posted away for the Army, and sends Letters to *Mustapha* to come to him, to purge himself from those Crimes, whereof he was formerly suspected, but now openly accused; if he could do it, he told him, he need not fear to approach his Presence. Upon the Receipt of this Letter, *Mustapha* was in a great Streight, if he should go to his Father, in such an angry Mood, he ran upon his Death; if he refused, that would be interpreted, as a plain Confession of the objected Crimes. Under this Dilemma, he resolved upon that course, which as it had more of Resolution in it, so it was fullest of Danger. Away goes he from *Amasia*, of which he was Governor, to his Father's Camp, which was pitch'd not far from the place. This he did either out of confidence of his own Innocency, or else presuming on the Assistance of the Army, if any Severity were meditated against him; whatever was the Motive of his Journey, this is certain, that he run unavoidably upon his own Destruction; For *Solyman* ever since he was at *Constantinople*, had resolved to put his Son to Death; and to make the Matter more plausible, he consulted the *Mufty*, (so the *Turks* call the chief of their Priests, as *Romanists* call theirs the Pope,) and that he might not speak to him in favour of *Mustapha*, he propounded to him a feign'd Case, thus, 'There was a Wealthy Merchant at *Constantinople*, who having occasion to Travel a long Journey from Home, left the care of his Family, his Wife and Children, and all his Affairs to a Slave of his, in whose Fidelity he put a great deal of Confidence; now this Slave, immediately after his departure, designed to destroy his Masters Wife and Children, committed to his Care, and Embezil his Estate, and to work against his Masters own Life, in case he should ever get him into his Power; What may be Lawfully done, said he, to the *Mufty*, with such a Slave.' *He deserves* says the *Mufty to be Rack'd to Death.* Whether he spoke really as he thought, or whither he did not do it to curry favour with *Rustan* and *Roxolana*; This is certain, that the Resolution of the *Grand Seignior* was greatly confirmed thereby to put his Son to Death, for he was of Opinion, *Mustapha*'s Offence against him, was as great, as that supposed Slaves against his Master. However it were, *Mustapha* came into his Fathers Camp, the whole Army being very sollicitous about the event of their Congress.

Soon after he was brought into his Fathers Tent, where all things were hush; not a Soldier of the Guards to be seen, no Serjeant, no Executioner in view, nor nothing of Treachery that was visible; but when he was come into an inner Tent, Lo! upon a sudden, there started up four Mutes, strong and lusty Fellows to be his Executioners; they set upon him with all their strength and might, and endeavoured to cast a Cord about his Neck; he defended himself stoutly for a while, (for he was a Robust young Man,) as if he had contended not only for Life, but for the Empire. For without Question, if he had escaped that danger, and had come in among the *Janizaries*, they either out of Affection to him, whom they dearly Loved; or else moved with the Indignity of the Thing, would not only have saved his Life, but have gone near to have Proclaimed him Emperor: And that was the very thing, which *Solyman* fear'd of all things in the World; and therefore perceiving, as he stood behind a Linnen Vail in the Tent to behold the Tragedy, that unexpected stop was put to his Bloody Design; he peep'd out his Head, and gave the Mutes such a sour and minacious Look, in reproach of their remisness; thereupon they assaulted him with renew'd Force, and then threw poor *Mustapha* down on the Ground, and Strangled him; and after they had done, they carried his Corps out of the Tent, and laid it on a piece of Tapestry, that so the *Janizaries* might behold their design'd Emperor.

As soon as the Matter was divulged, Commiseration and Grief seized on the whole Camp, and there was scarce a Man of any Consideration in the whole Army, that did not approach to behold so sad a Spectacle, especially the *Janizaries*, whose Confirmation and Rage was such, that they would have ventured to attempt any Manner of Mischief whatsoever, if they had had a Leader. As for him whom they hoped to be their Conductor, he lay dead on the Ground, and therefore now there was no Way but one, to take that patiently which was past all Remedy.

Thus they silently departed with blubber'd Eyes, and sad Hearts, to their Tents, where they both lamented and pitied the woful Fate of unhappy *Mustapha*, sometimes inveighing against the Madness and Rage of his old doating Father, at other Times exclaiming at the Fraud and Cruelty of his Step-Mother, and anon cursing the Wickedness of *Rustan*, with direful

Imprecations for extinguishing so great a Light of the *Ottoman* Family, so that all that Day was a Fasting-day to them, they did not sip so much as a drop of Water; yea, some of them continued their Abstinence for many Days after. In short, there was such a Face of Mourning over the whole Army, which was not like to cease in many Days, that *Solyman* in Policy, and in a seeming Compliance with the Sentiments of his People, deprived *Rustan* of his Office (it being thought by his own Consent) and Banished him, as a private Person to *Constantinople*, substituting *Achmat* Bashaw to the *Grand-Vizier-ship* in his Room, a Man of more Courage than Conduct.

UPON this Alteration, the public Grief was somewhat abated, and the Soldiers Rage pacified; for the Commonalty was made to believe, That *Solyman* at last had found out the Wickedness of *Rustan*, and the Inchantments of his Wife; and that now he repented, though it were late, first of his Cruelty to *Mustapha*. and thereupon had banished *Rustan* from his Presence, and that he would not spare his Wife neither, as soon as he came to *Constantinople*. As for *Rustan*, he pretended great Sorrow, and departed to *Constantinople*, without seeming to have the least hope, ever to be restored to his former Dignity.

BUT alas! *Roxolana* was not content with the Destruction of *Mustapha*, as long as he had an only Son, who was yet in his Minority, alive; for she did not think her own, or her Childrens Security, to be sufficiently provided for, as long as any of *Mustapha*'s Race were alive; but she wanted a fair pretence to accomplish her Design, nor was it long before she found One. She represented to *Solyman*, that as often as his Grand-child, *Mustapha*'s Son went abroad at *Prusa*, where he was brought up, the Youth of that City were wont to flock about him, to wish him all Happiness, and particularly to pray, *That he might long survive his Father*. And whither (said she) can this tend, but to prompt him to mount the Throne, and revenge his Father's Death? And to be sure, the *Janizaries* will take his Part, (added She;) and thus the Death of *Mustapha* alone, will add little Security to the public Peace and Tranquility. Religion (proceeded she) is to be preferred before even the Lives of our own Children; and seeing that of the *Musselmans*, (for so they call their Religion, as counting it the best) stands and falls with the *Ottoman* Family; if that House fail, farewel Religion also. And how can that House stand, if Domestic Discord undermine it? And therefore Sir, if you prevent the Ruin of your House, your Empire and your Religion, you must use all manner of means; nay, you must not stick at Parricide itself; if homebred Disagreement and Feud may be thereby prevented; for the safety of Religion will over-ballance the Loss, even of a Man's own Children. As for *Mustapha*'s Son, you have the less Reason to spare him, because his Father's Crime hath already infected him, and there is do doubt, but, if he be suffered to Live, he will soon endeavour to Head a Party, to revenge his Father's Death.

BY these Reasons *Solyman* was induced to yield to the Murder of his Grandchild, and thereupon sent *Ebrahim* Bashaw to *Prusa*, to destroy the innocent Youth. As soon as the Bashaw came thither, he made it his great Business to conceal his intended Design from the Child's Mother; for, he thought, it would be look'd upon as an inhuman Thing in him, to cut off a Youth, with the Privity of his Mother, and, as it were, before her Eyes. And, besides, he was afraid the People would rise in Arms upon the Perpetration of so cruel a Fact; and therefore at first, Fox like, he sets his Wits at work to deceive the Mother. He pretended that he was sent by *Solyman*, out of Respect to her and her Son, to visit them; that his Master saw his Error in putting his Son to Death, which he now, too late repented of; but that the crueller he had been to the Father, the more indulgent he would be to his Son; and many such colloguing Words he used, whereby he imposed upon the too credulous Mother, who was the rather induced to believe him, because of *Rustan*'s Disgrace and Fall; and to crown his Flattery, he presented them with many Gifts. This past on for a Day or two, and then some Discourse was administred concerning their going abroad, out of the City, to enjoy the fresh Air. And the Bashaw, being an Eunuch, persuaded her the next Day to take a Turn in the Suburbs, she in her Coach, and himself, with her Son, would ride afore on Horseback. The Matter seemed not to afford any Suspicion, and therefore she consented, and a Chariot is prepared for her; but (mark the Fraud!) the Axle-Tree of the Coach was so made, on Purpose, that it must needs break, when it came to be jogged in any rough Way. Thus she, in an unlucky Time, began her Journey out of the City. The Eunuch and the Child rode a pretty Way before, as if they had Occasion for some private Discourse, and the Mother speeded after as fast as she was able; but when the Coach came to the designed craggy Place, the Wheel violently hit against the Rocks, and so the Axle-Tree broke. This the Mother looked upon as an unlucky Omen, and therefore, in a great Fright, she could not long be restrained from leaving her Coach, and with a few of her Maids, from following her Son on Foot. But, alas! 'twas too late; for the Eunuch being come to the House designed for the Slaughter, without any more ado, shewed the Child the Emperor's Mandate for his Death. He answered, according to the Principles of their Religion, That he looked upon that Command as proceeding not from the Emperor, but from God, which must necessarily be obeyed, and so he yielded his Neck to the Bow-String.

THUS died this innocent and hopeful Youth. When the Eunuch had perpetrated this wicked Fact, he stole out at a Back-door, and fled as fast as he could. The Mother, soon after, beginning to smell out the Fraud, knocks at the Door; when they thought fit they opened it, and there she saw her Son sprawling on the Ground, his Breath being yet hardly out of his Body. Here let me draw a Vail; for a Mother's Affection to a Son in such a lamentable Juncture, may be better conceived than expressed. Upon this dismal Sight she was hurried back to *Prusa*, where she tore her Hair, rent her Garments, filled the whole Town with Howlings, Moans, &c. The *Prusian* Ladies, with their Daughters and Waiting-Maids, came in Multitudes to her, and were stark Mad to hear of so great a Butchery; and running in that raving Manner out of the Gates, all the Cry was, *Where's the Eunuch? Where's the Eunuch? Let's have him to tear him to pieces*: But he foreseeing what would happen, and fearing, like another *Orpheus*, to be torn Peace-meal by those raging Furies, had cunningly withdrawn himself.

BUT to return to my Purpose. As soon as I came to *Constantinople*, Letters were sent to *Solyman*, then at *Amasia*, to acquaint him with my Arrival; and, till his Answer was return'd, I had Leisure to take a View of the City of *Constantinople*; and first, I had a Mind to visit the Temple of St. *Sophia*, which I was not admitted to do, but by special Favour; for the *Turks* think that their Temples are prophaned, if a *Christian* do but put his Foot within them.

THAT Church is a magnificent Pile, and a worthy Structure to behold. It hath a great Arch or Hemisphere in the Middle, which hath no Light but only from the Sky: All the *Turkish Mosks* are built after the Form of this. Some say, that heretofore it was much larger, and contained many Apartments, which were all destroyed by the *Turks*, and only the *Quire* and *Nave*, in the Middle of it, standing.

As for the Situation of the City itself, it seemed to me, to be naturally placed as fit to be the Mistress of the World; it stands in *Europe*, and hath *Asia* in view, and on its right, hath *Egypt* and *Africa*; which, though Countries not adjacent to it, yet by reason of frequent Intercourse and Naval Commerce, they seem as it were, contiguous. On its left Hand is the *Euxin Sea*, and the *Palus Mœtis*, whose Banks are inhabited round about by many Nations, and so many navigable Rivers have their Influx into them, that there is nothing grows in any of the Countries thereabout, fit for Man's Use; but there is a great Conveniency of transporting it by Sea to *Constantinople*.

On the one Side, it is wash'd with the *Propontis*; on the other, the River makes an Haven, which *Strabo* calls, The Golden Horn, from the Similitude it hath to an Horn; on the other Side, it is joined to the rest of the Continent, so that it almost resembles a Peninsule; and with the continued back of a Promontory, it runs out into the Sea and a Bay, which is made there by the River and the Sea. So that from the middle of *Constantinople*, there is a most pleasant Prospect into the Sea, and even to the Mount *Olympus*, in *Asia*, which bears a snowy Head all the Year long. The Sea there, is wonderful full of Fish, which sometimes swim down from the *Mœotis* and the *Euxine*, through the *Bosphorus* and *Propontis*, into the *Ægœan* and *Mediterranean Seas*, and sometimes they swim from thence into the *Euxin*, according to the Nature of the Fish; and that in Shoals so thick and numerous, that you may catch them with your Hands. So that here is excellent fishing for *Mackrel, Tunny, Cod, Porpois* and *Sword-Fish*. But the *Greeks* fish more than the *Turks*, though these latter love Fish well enough; provided, they be of the Number of those, which they count *clean*; as for others, they had rather eat Poison than taste them, for a *Turk* had rather his Tongue or his Teeth were pluck'd out of his Head, than taste of any Thing they think to be *unclean*, as a *Frog*, a *Snail*, or a *Tortoise*. And herein, the *Greeks* are every jot as Superstitious as they; of which I will give you the Instance following.

I entertain'd in my Family, a Youth of the *Greek* Religion; I employed him as my Steward. The rest of my Servants could never persuade him to eat any *Periwinkles* or *Cockles*; but at last, they put a Trick upon him; they caused them to be so high-season'd and disguis'd, that he, mistaking them for another sort of Fish, fed upon them most heartily. Whereupon, my People set up a Laughter, and threw down the Shells before him, where by he perceiv'd himself to be cozen'd: Whereupon, 'tis incredible to relate how much he was troubled. He went presently to his Chamber, and there fell a Vomiting, Weeping, and Afflicting himself most grievously, without any Intermission; insomuch, that two Months Sallary was not sufficient to expiate this Offence; for that's the Guise of *Greek* Priests, according to the kind and greatness of the Offence, they lay a pecuniary Mulct upon those who come to *Confess*, and they never *Absolve* them till they pay it down to a Penny.

In the furthest Point of that Promontory which I mentioned before, stands the Palace, or *Seraglio*, of the *Turkish* Emperors: To me, it did not seem very magnificent, either for Work or Workmanship (for you must know, that as yet, I had not made an Entrance into it.) Under the Palace, in a low Ground, and as it were, upon the Sea-shore, are the Gardens of the *Grand Seignior*, where the greatest Part of *Old Bysantium* is thought to have stood.

I hope you do not expect to be informed by me, why the *Chalcedonians*, who built a City over-against *Byzantium* (the Ruins whereof are yet to be seen) were Sirnam'd *The Blind*; nor shall I tell you the Nature of that Sea, which always runs downward with a vast Stream, but never recoils with any Tide; nor will I spend Time to speak of those *Hautgis* which were brought to *Constantinople* from the *Palus Mæotis*, such as the *Italians* call *Moronella's Botargues* and *Caviare*; the Description of all these Particulars would swell my Epistle to too great a Bulk, and besides, it would be needless; for both the *Antients*, and also *Modern* Writers, have given Information of those Particulars at large.

To return then to the Site of *Constantinople*. There is no Place in the World more pleasantly seated to the Eye, nor more convenient for Trade. But, let me tell you, the Buildings therein (as in all other *Turkish* Cities) are not magnificent, nor are their Streets stately or large; nay, in *Constantinople*, they are so narrow, that they much eclipse the Beauty of the Place. Yet there are in it some valuable Relicks of old Monuments to be seen; but not so many as a Man would imagine, considering how many *Constantine* brought thither from *Rome*. It is not my Purpose to insist upon each of these Particulars; yet, a Word or two of the principal ones.

In the *Area* of the old *Hippodrome*, there are two Serpents cut in Brass; as also, a mighty *Obelisk*. Moreover, *Constantinople* doth gratifie us with the Sight of two memorable Pillars; *One* over-against the *Caravaserai*, where I lodged, and the *Other* in the *Forum*, called by the *Turks, Auratbasar*, i. e. *The Womens Court*, wherein, from Bottom to Top, is engraven the History of a certain Expedition of one *Arcadius*, who built it, and whose Statue, for a long time, stood on the Top of it. And yet it may rather be called a *Stair-Case*, than a *Pillar*, because it goes winding up like a Pair of Stairs. I caused the Shape of this Pillar to be drawn, which I have by me. But the other Pillar, over-against the House the *German* Ambassadors used to lodge in, the whole Structure, besides the Basis and the Chapiter, consists of eight solid Marble or Red *Porphyry* Stones, so curiously joined together, that they seem but one continued Stone. For, where the Stones are jointed one into another, upon that Commissure, there is wrought a circular Garland of Lawrels round about the Pillar, which hides the jointing, so that they which look upon it from the Ground, perceive no jointing at all. That Pillar hath been so often shaken by Earthquakes, and so battered by Fires happening near it, that it is cleft in many Places, and they are forced to bind it about with Iron Hoops, that it may not fall to pieces.

THEY say, That the Statue of *Apollo* once stood upon that Pillar, and that afterwards the Statues of *Constantine*, and of *Theodosius* the Elder, were erected there; but they are all thrown down, either by the Force of the Winds, or by Earthquakes.

THE *Greeks* tell this Story concerning the *Obelisk*, in the *Hippodrome*, which I mentioned before, *viz.*

THAT it fell from its Basis, and lay for many Ages upon the Ground; but in the Time of the later Emperors, there was an Architect found, who undertook to raise it up to its Place; but he demanded a vast Reward for his Pains. After the Price was agreed on, he prepared abundance of Ropes, Pullies, and other Instruments, and by those means, he lifted up that vast Stone, within one Inch of the Place where it was to stand; but his present *Apparatus* being able to raise it no higher, the People, who in great Numbers were his Spectators, were of Opinion, that all his former Cost and Pains were lost, and he must begin anew to try to do the Feat some other way, to his vast Expence and Charge. The Artist himself was not discouraged; but being skilful in *Mechanick Philosophy*, he caused abundance of Water to be brought up to him, which, for many Hours, he cast upon the Ropes, to which the *Obelisk* hung; and those Ropes, being often wet and dry, shrunk a little, and by that means, lifted up the Weight to its designed Station, to the great Admiration and Applause of the Vulgar.

AT *Constantinople* I saw several Sorts of wild Beasts, such as *Lynxes*, *Cat-a-Mountains*, *Panthers*, *Leopards*, and *Lyons*; but they were so gentle and tame, that I saw one of the Keepers pull a *Sheep* out of a *Lyon*'s Mouth, so that he only moistened his Jaws with the Blood, without devouring it. I saw also a young *Elephant*, so wanton, that he would dance, and play at Ball. Sure you cannot chuse but laugh, when I tell you of an *Elephant*'s dancing and playing at Ball; but if I should say no more, why may you not believe me as well as *Seneca*, who tells us of one that could dance upon the Rope? Or as *Pliny*, who speaks of another that understood *Greek*? But that you may not think me an egregious Forger, give me leave to explain myself: When this *Elephant* was bid to dance, he did so caper or quaver with his whole Body, and interchangeably move his Feet, that he seemed to represent a kind of a Jig; and as for playing at Ball, he very prettily took up the Ball in his Trunk, and sent it packing therewith, as we do with the Palm of the Hand.

AMONG those wild Beasts, there had been a *Camelopardalis*, but she died a little before I came to *Constantinople*; however, I caused her Bones, which had been buried in the Earth, to be digged up, that I might inspect the Make of this Creature. It is an Animal a great deal taller in the Forepart than in the Hinder; and, for that Reason, it is unfit to carry a Man, or any other Burden. It hath an Head and a Neck like a *Camel*, but a spotted Skin like a *Leopard*, and therefore it is called by a Name derived from both, (*i. e.*) *Camelopardalis*.

IT might have been imputed as a Piece of great Neglect in me, not to have visited the *Euxine*, especially as I had an Opportunity of sailing thither; seeing the Ancients used to account it as great a Piece of Curiosity to see *Pontus*, as to visit *Corinth*. Thither, therefore, I sailed with a prosperous Gale, and had the Privilege to be admitted into some of the Pleasure-Houses of the *Grand Seignior*.

IN the Valves of one of them, I beheld the famous Fight of *Selimus* with *Ishmael* King of the *Persians*, excellently described in Checker-Work. I had also the View of many of the Orchards and Groves of the *Turkish* Emperor, which were seated in most pleasant Vallies. This I may say of them, That they ow'd little to Art, but almost all to Nature; so that I could not chuse but entertain such *Epiphonema's* as these in my Thoughts, O most pleasant Houses for Nymphs! O choise Seats for the Muses! O Retirements fit for the Learned! To deal plainly with you (as I told you before) they seemed to me, as it were, sensibly to bewail their present Posture, and to cry aloud to *Christians* for their better Cultivation; and not they only, but much more *Constantinople* itself, yea, and all *Greece* too; which being, heretofore, the most flourishing Country in the World, is now wofully enslaved by *Barbarians*. Formerly it was the Mother and Nurse of all good Arts and liberal Sciences, but now, alas! it seems to call for that Culture and Humanity which once it delivered down to us; and, by Way of Requital, claims the Redemption of our common Religion from that *Scythian Barbarism* under which it groans; and call it may long enough, for (with Grief may we speak it) *Christian* Princes, now a-days, are otherwise employed; so that the *Turks* do not more domineer over the poor *Greeks*, than Vices, such as Luxury, Gluttony, Sloth, Lust, Pride, *&c.* do over *Christians*, which so clog, enervate, and depress our Minds, that we can hardly look Heaven-ward, or aspire to any Thing that is truly Great and Excellent.

METHINKS, Duty and Piety should have been sufficient Motives to us to help our afflicted Brethren; but if we had been proof against those Incentives, so that neither brave nor praise-worthy Actions could unthaw our frozen Courage; yet Profit and Advantage, which are now the great Bias of the World, might have stirred us up to recover such opulent and commodious Countries from Infidels, and to possess them ourselves: But, on the contrary, we plow the Ocean, even as far as the *Indies*, and the very *Antipodes*, because there we get rich Prey and Spoil at a cheap Rate, even without Bloodshed, by imposing on the simple and uncrafty *Indians*. 'Tis true, we pretend the Conversion of the *Heathens*, but, if we go to the Root of the Matter, (to our Shame be it spoken) 'tis their Gold, not their Godliness, is the Gain we seek for. Our Ancestors carried it at quite another Rate, who did not, like trading Merchants, seek after those Places where there was most Wealth, but where there was greater Opportunity for noble and virtuous Atchievements; so that it was not Profit, but Honour, which put them upon hazardous and remote Expeditions: And when they came home, they were more laden with Glory than with Plunder. I speak this in your Ear; for others, perhaps, may think it a peculiar thing in me, to detract from the Manners of the present Age. But, let them think what they will, I see that the Arrow is drawn to the Head to destroy us; and I am afraid, that we, who would not fight for Glory, shall be forced to do it to save our Lives. But to return to *Pontus*.

THE *Turks* call the *Euxine, Caradenis,* (i. e.) *The Black Sea.* It falls down thro' narrow Streights into the *Thracian Bosphorus*, where its Waters are tossed up and down by many Vortices, Turnings, and Windings, occasioned by several Promontories jutting out into it; and thus, in one Day's Passage, it descends to *Constantinople*, and from thence, almost by the like strait Passage, it breaks out into the *Propontis*. In the Middle of the Bay, where it makes its Influx into the *Bosphorus*, there is a Rock with an erected Pillar, in the Basis whereof is writ the Name of a certain *Roman*, called *Octavian*, (if my Memory fail not) in *Latin* Letters.

ON the *European* Shore there is a Tower, called *Pharos*, where they hang out Lights in the Night, to guide Sailors by. Not far from this Place, a River falls into the Sea, in the Channel whereof there are found Stones, little inferior to *Onyxes* or *Sardonyxes*, and, if they be polished, are as shining as they. A few Miles from that Bay, which I lately spoke of, we may see those Streights over which *Darius* wasted his Army against the *European Scythians*: And about the Middle, between the two Mouths of the *Bosphorus*, there are two Castles, one of which is in *Europe*, and the other on the opposite Shore, in *Asia*. This latter was possessed by the *Turks* long before *Mahomet* took *Constantinople*. The other was built by him some few Years after he became Master of that City. The *Turks* make use of it, at this Day, as a Prison for the nobler Sort of their Captives. *Lazarus*, a Commander, or Prince of the *Epitots* not long ago was taken Prisoner by the *Turks*, together with some *Spaniards* at *Castlenovo*, and committed to this Tower; from whence making his Escape, and being retaken, he was impal'd, (*i. e.*) put to a most cruel Death, by having a Pole thrust thro' his Body, from his Fundament to his very Neck; yet he indured it with incredible Patience.

PERHAPS you expect that I should here give you an Account of those floating Islands, called *Cyaneæ* or *Symplegades*. But, to deal freely with you, those few Hours that I spent on the *Pontus*, I saw no such Islands at all; whether they had been carried to any other Place, I know not: If you desire to have a more particular Information concerning them, you may consult *Peter Gyllius*, who was an exact Enquirer into such Curiosities; for my Part, I shall record only what I saw, or know to be true. Yet I think it is not fit for me to conceal a Mistake that *Polybius* is guilty of; for he proposes many Arguments, to prove that, in Tract of Time, the *Euxine* will be choaked up with Sand and other Trash, brought in by the *Danow*, the *Borysthenes*, and other great Rivers falling into it, that it would be made unfit for Navigation; whereas, the contrary appeared to me; for that Sea is every jot as navigable, at this Day, as it was of old in the Days of *Polybius*. And though he seemed to have some Grounds for his Opinion, that to him were irrefragable, yet Time hath shewed them to be weak. The like Observation holds in other Cases; for, of old, who would not believe the Ancients, who affirmed, upon seemingly imaginable Grounds, That the Torrid Zone was inhabitable? whereas, later Discoveries have fully convinced us, That those hot Countries are as well inhabited as any other Part of the Terrestial Globe; nay, when the Sun is at the highest with them, and darts down its Rays perpendicularly upon them; even at that very Time the Ardency of the Heat is so tempered and cooled by continued Rains, that those Countries are rendered very fit for human Habitations. But to return.

After the *Grand Seignior* was informed, by Letters, of my Arrival (as I said before) he sent to the Governor of *Constantinople*, intimating his Pleasure, that he should send us to him into *Asia*, as far as the City of *Amasia*, or (as it is writ on ancient Coins) *Amazeia*, where he then was. Upon this Advice we prepared all Things for our Journey; and, with our Guides, on the 9th of *March* we were wafted over into *Natolia*, (for so the *Turks* call *Asia* at this Day.) That Day we went no farther than *Scutari*, a Town on the *Asiatick* Shore, opposite to Old *Byzantium*; where, or very little above it, the noble City of *Chalcedon* was formerly thought to stand. The *Turks* were of Opinion, That when our Horses, Coaches, Baggage, and Train, together with ourselves, were all got over the *Hellespont*, 'twas enough for one Day's Journey; especially considering, that if we had forgot any of the necessary Accoutrements for our Journey, or had left them behind at *Constantinople*, (as it sometimes happened) we might bethink ourselves before we went any farther, and fetch them over. The next Day we continued our Journey from *Scutari*, over fragrant Fields, full of odoriferous Plants, and especially *Stœchas's*, a sweet smelling Spike. There we saw a vast Number of *Tortoises*, stalking over all the Field, without any Fear at all. We had certainly seized upon a great many of them, as a Prey grateful to our Palates, had it not been for our *Turkish* Guides, whom we were afraid to disoblige; for if they had seen any of them brought to our Table, much more, if they had touched them, they would have thought themselves so defiled, that I know not how many Washings would not have cleansed their imagined Pollution. For, as I told you before, the *Turks*, and the *Greeks* too, are so superstitious, that they abhor ever to touch of that Animal; so that, it being no hurtful Creature, and no body endeavouring to catch them, the whole Country abounds with *Tortoises*. I kept one of them by me a great while, which had two Heads, and it would have lived much longer, if I had been as careful of it as I might. That Day's Journey brought us to a Village, called *Cartaly*, which I mention, because I shall, for the future, gratify you with the Knowledge of the several Stages of this Voyage. For tho' the Journey from *Vienna* to *Constantinople* hath been performed by many, yet this from *Constantinople* to *Amasia*, hath, as yet, been undergone by no *Christian* that I know of. From *Cartaly* we came to *Gabise*, a Town of *Bithynia*, which some think was anciently called *Libyssa*, and is famous for the Sepulchre of *Hannibal*, who was there interred. From thence there is a most pleasant Prospect into the Sea, and into the Bay of *Nicomedia*; here also grow *Cyprus* Trees of a wonderful Bulk and Tallness.

Our fourth Day's Journey from *Constantinople* brought us to *Nicomedia*, a City, anciently of great Note; but we saw nothing remarkable in it, but the Ruins and Rubbish of old Walls, with some broken Pieces of Pillars with their Chapiters, which were all the Remainders of its ancient Splendor, except one Castle on an Hill, which was somewhat more entire. A little before we came to this Place, some Workmen, that were digging under Ground, discovered a long Wall made with Marble, which (it may be) was part of the ancient Palace of the Kings of *Bithynia*.

From *Nicomedia*, we passed over a Cliff or Ridge of Mount *Olympus*, and came to a Village called *Kasockly*, and from thence to *Nice*; but it was so late before we came thither, that the first Watch was set. Not far from that Place, I heard a mighty Noise, as if it had been of Men that jeer'd and mock'd us. I asked what was the Matter? Whether any of the Mariners, rowing on the Lake *Ascanius*, (which was not far off) did deride us, for travelling at that unusual Time of Night? I was answered, No, but it was only the howling of certain Beasts, which the *Turks* call *Ciacals*, or *Jacals*. They are a Sort of Wolves, somewhat bigger than Foxes, but less than common Wolves; yet as greedy and devouring as the most ravenous Wolves or Foxes of all. They go in Flocks, and seldom or never hurt either Man or Beast, but get their Food by Craft and Stealth, more than by open Force. Thence it is, that the *Turks* call subtle and crafty Persons, especially the *Asiaticks*, by the Metaphorical Name of *Ciacals*. Their Manner is to enter into the Tents or Houses of the *Turks*, in the Night-Time, and what they can catch that is eatable, that they eat; and if they find nothing else to devour, then they fall a gnawing of all Kinds of Leather Things, as Shoes, Boots, Girdles, Scabbards of Swords, and the like; and they are as cunning as they are thievish; but in this they are very ridiculous, that they discover themselves by the Noise they make. For whilst they are most busy in a House, devouring their Prey, if any one of their Herd, that stays without Doors, chance to howl, they all set up a howling likewise; and thus, forgetting where they are, they raise up the People of the House, who leap out of their Beds, and cudgel them soundly.

ALL the next Day we staid at *Nice*; I believe my Lodging was in the same House where the Council of *Nice* was heretofore celebrated. As for the Town itself, it is seated on the Bank of the Lake *Ascanius*. The Walls of it are almost entire, so are the Gates, which are but four, and may all may be seen from the Middle of the Market-Place; in each of them there were old Inscriptions in *Latin*, which shew that the Town was repaired by *Antoninus*: which of them I do not well remember; but sure it must be by *Antoninus* the Emperor. There are also some Remainders of his Baths, and whilst the *Turks* were digging out Stones from thence to build Houses at *Constantinople*, they found the Statue of a Soldier in his Armour, curiously wrought, and almost entire; but they quickly battered it with their Hammers, even in our View; and when we shewed ourselves displeased at their rude Violence, they paid us with a Jeer, *What*, said the Labourers, *will you bow down to worship this Statue, as you* Christians *used to do to yours?*

FROM *Nice* we continued our Journey to a Place called *Jenysar*. From *Jenysar* to *Ackbyuck*, from *Ackbyuck* to *Bazargyck*, from *Bazargyck* to *Bosowick*, otherwise called *Cassumbasa*, seated in the narrowest Streights of Mount *Olympus*; for almost all our Way from *Nice* thither, lay through the Cliff of that Mountain. At *Nice* we lodged in a *Turkish* Inn, or Hospital, and just against it was a Rock, standing on high Ground, wherein there was a square deep Trench cut, and from the Bottom thereof there issued out a

Canal, that reached to the Highway. That Trench or Ditch, the ancient Inhabitants of that Place used, in the Winter Time, to fill with Snow; that so the melted Snow-Water gently dropping down into the Road, by the fore-mentioned Canal, might quench the Thirst of parched Travellers. Such Works as these the *Turks* count *Eleemosynary* ones; because they are for the publick Benefit and Advantage of Mankind.

Not far from this Place, on the Right Hand, we saw a Town, called *Otmanlick*, borrowing its Name, (as I conceive) from *Ottoman*, the Founder of the *Ottoman* Family, who lived there.

From those Streights we descended into an open Campaign; and when we came thither, we lay the first Night in our Tents, whereby the Heat did not so much incommode us, as otherwise it would have done; the Place was called *Chiausada*. The most remarkable Things we saw here, was a subterraneous House, that had no Light, but only what stole in at the Roof: We saw also that Sort of *Goats*, of whose Hair, (or Fleece, if you had rather call it so) they make the Shagreen or watered Stuff, called Camlet. If you would know the Nature of that Creature, I shall not entertain you with a Flam, but give you the true Description of it.

The Hair of this Creature is very fine, and extreamly white, and it hangs down from their Bodies to the Ground. The Goat-herds do not sheer, but kemb it off, and it is almost as fine as Silk. These *Goats* are often washed in the neighbouring Rivers, and feed upon the Grass growing there, which is very tender and dry, and that certainly contributes much to the Fineness of their Wool; for if they are removed to another Place, their Fleece changes with their Pasture, and their Kids do so degenerate, that one would hardly think them of the same Breed. The Thread that is spun of that Hair or Wool, is carried, by the Women of that Country, to *Ancyra*, a City of *Galatia*, where it is woven into Cloth and dy'd, as I shall tell you anon.

Moreover the Sheep of those Countries have very fat and weighty Tails, (their Sheep-Flocks consist hardly of any other.) The Tail of any one of them weighs sometimes three or four Pound, and sometimes eight or ten; yea, they grow so big in some old Sheep, that they are forc'd to lay them upon a Plank, running on two little Wheels, that so they may draw them after them, not being otherwise able to trail them along.

Perhaps you will think I tell you a Romance; but, take it on my Word, it is a certain Truth. I grant, such bulky Tails may be of some Advantage, because they are full of Fat; but the Flesh of the Sheep seemed more harsh and rank to me, than our own Mutton. The Shepherds that tend them lie Day and Night in the Fields, and carry their Wives and Children about with them, in Waggons, which serve them instead of Houses; only sometimes they erect small Tents to lie under. They wander far and near, sometimes in the open Campaign, sometimes over Hills, sometimes over Dales, as the Season of the Year, and the Necessity of Pasturage, doth require.

I saw also in those Countries, some Sort of Birds, unknown to us, and such as I never saw before. Among the rest, there is a Kind of *Ducks*, which gives a Sound like Trumpeters, or such as blow the Cornet; the Noise they make is almost like the Sound of a Post-Boy's Horn. It is a Bird, which though it hath nothing wherewith to defend itself, yet is very strong and daring.

The *Turks* are verily persuaded, that the Devils are afraid of these Birds. This is certain, they are so tenaciously sensible of their Liberty, that tho' they have been kept up tame in a Coop, for three Years together, yet if they can but get an Opportunity to escape away, they fly to their wonted Haunts, as preferring their natural Seats before their confined Prisons, though they be cramm'd and fatten'd there.

We passed on from *Chiousada* to *Karali*; from *Karali* to *Hazdengri*; from thence to *Mazotthoy*; from *Mazotthoy* we passed over the River *Sangar*, which runs into *Pontus* out of *Phrygia*, and came to *Mahathli*, from thence to *Zugli*, thence to *Chilancyck*; from *Chilancyck* to *Ialancich*; from thence to *Portughin*; and from *Portughin* we reached to *Ancyra*, called by the *Turks*, *Angur*. We staid one whole Day at *Ancyra*, partly because the *Turks* did not hasten us; for, in regard the *Persian* Embassador made an Halt, we were desired to do so too, that we might make our Entrances, both at one Time, into *Amasia*. I saw nothing remarkable in all the Villages aforementioned, save that sometimes, among the *Turkish* Sepulchres, we happened to see some Pillars, or ancient Stones of curious Marble, wherein there were several Remains of *Latin* or *Greek* Inscriptions, but so defaced, that they could not be read; which Disappointment I very much resented, for all my Delight was, as soon as I came to my Inn at Night, to enquire after old Inscriptions, together with *Latin* and *Greek* Coins; and sometimes for rare Kinds of Plants.

As for the Sepulchres, or Graves of the *Turks*, their Custom is, not to fill them with Earth, but throw great Stones upon them for a Covering. Would you know the Reason? 'tis Superstitious enough. The *Turks* believe, that whenever the Devil accuses the Deceased, and calls upon him to give an Account how he spent his Life; then his good Genius will defend him, and this Stone is the Place upon which the Ghost must sit, that he may plead his Cause with more Care; and it is so huge and bulky, that Dogs, Wolves, or other ravenous Beasts, especially the *Hyænæ*, may not injure his Corps as it lies in the Earth.

The *Hyæna* is a Beast common in these Countries; she uses to dig up Graves, and taking out the dead Bodies from thence, carries them to her Den, near which you shall see a great Heap of Bones of Men, Horses, and other Creatures. She is a little lower than a Wolf, and quite as long; she hath a Skin like a Wolf, only her Hair is rougher and full of great black Spots; her Head is contiguous to her *Spina dorsi*, without any *vertebræ* at all; so that, when she looks backward, she must of necessity turn her whole Body: Instead of a Row of Teeth, she hath but one continued Bone. The *Turks* do ascribe great Vertue to this Beast, in *Philtres*, as did the Antients: there were two of them at *Constantinople*, when I was there; I cheapned them, but their Owners were unwilling to sell them, because they kept them for the *Sultaness*, who was thought, by Love-Portions, and Magic Art, to have engaged her Husband's Love to her. Here I cannot chuse but take Notice of a Mistake in *Bellonius*, who thinks the *Hyæna* to be the same Creature with that we call the *Zibeth* or *Musk-Cat*.

The *Turks* have a Tradition, that the *Hyæna*, which they call *Zirtlan*, understands what Men say one to another. The Antients affirm'd, that they could also imitate Man's Voice, and thereupon Hunters catch them by this Wile. They find out her Den, which they may easily do by the heap of Bones lying by it; and then one of them goes in with a Rope, leaving the other End of the Rope in the Hands of his Fellows without; and when he is creeping in, he cries with a loud Voice, *Joctur, Joctur, Ucala!* i. e. *She is not here, She is not here!* or, *I cannot find her!* whereupon, the *Hyæna*, thinking she is not discovered, lies close, and he ties one end of the Rope about her Leg; and then he goes forth, still crying, *I cannot find her!* but when he is escaped quite out of the Hole, he cries out aloud, *She is within, She is within!* which the *Hyæna* hearing, and understanding the meaning of it, leaps out, thinking to escape; but then they hold her back by the Rope, tied to her Leg, and either kill her, or, if they use Care and Diligence, lake her alive, for she is a fierce Creature, and defends herself desperately.

I found abundance of Old Coins all up and down this Country, especially of the later Emperors, *viz.* the *Constantines*, the *Constantius*'s, the *Justin*'s, the *Valens*'s, the *Valentine*'s, the *Numerian*'s, the *Probus*'s, the *Tacitus*'s, and such like. In many Places the *Turks* use them for Weight, *viz.* of a Drachm, or half a Drachm; and they call it *Giaur Manguri*, i. e. the Money of the *Pagans* or *Infidels*. The like Coins I found in the neighbouring Cities of *Asia*, as at *Amysus*, at *Synopis*, at *Cumana*, at *Amastris*, and *Amasia* itself, whither we were going. There was a Brasier of that City which grieved me very much; for demanding of him, whether he had any Old Coins to sell? He answered me, That a few Days ago, he had a large Room full of them, but had melted them down to make Brass Kettles, as thinking them of little Value, and fit for no other Use. When I heard this Story, it troubled me much to lose so many choice Monuments of Antiquity; but I paid him back in his own Coin, by telling; him, That I would have given him a hundred Guilders for them; so that my Revenge was suited to his Injury; for I sent him away as sorrowful, as he did me for losing the Coins.

As for Plants, I saw very few in my Journey in those Parts, which were unknown to us in *Europe*. They were almost all of the same Kind; only they were more or less flourishing, according to the Richness or Poverty of the Soil. The *Amomum*, which, *Dioscorides* says, grows near *Pontus*, I very diligently sought for, but in vain; so that I knew not whether that Plant did not fail in that Country, or else was transplanted into another.

This Town of *Ancyra*, was our 9th Stage from *Constantinople*. It is a Town of *Galatia*, sometimes the Seat of the *Gauls*, called by *Pliny*, *Tectosagum*; nor was it unknown to *Strabo*: Though perhaps the present Town is but part of the old Town, called in the Canons, *Anguira*. Here we saw a stately Superscription, and a Sampler of those Tables, wherein the Atchievments of *Augustus* were summarily comprehended. I caused as much of it, as we could read, to be transcribed. It is cut in the Marble Walls of that Structure, which heretofore was the Town-hall; but is now demolished, so that one part of it is visible to those that enter on the right

Hand, and the other to those that enter upon the left. The top Chapiters are almost entire; the Middle is full of Clefts, and the lowermost Part of it is so battered with Clubs and Hatchets, that it cannot be read; which Loss cannot be sufficiently lamented by all Lovers of Learning; and so much the more, because the Commons of *Asia*, dedicated this City to *Augustus*. Here also, we were Eye-witnesses of the dying of that Cloth, I spake of before, made of Goats-wool, and how they Camlet it, or give it its Water-colour; 'tis done thus. They pour Water upon it, and by means of a Cloth-press, cause it to receive that Colour. That is counted the best, which is most variegated in every part; and if, in any Piece, the Water-colours do not deeply and uniformly appear, that Piece, though of the same Colour, and made of the same Wool, is valued at some Gilders less than another, because it is not so deeply tinctured. The better sort of *Turks*, in their old Age, are usually clothed with this Sort of Cloth, and *Solyman* himself used to wear Vests of it; but Green is a Colour disused much by *Christians*; and the rather, because the *Turks* commend it upon a Superstituous Account, as being worn by their Prophet *Mahomet* in his older Days.

A black Colour is counted unfortunate, and is disliked by them; and, when they see any Man so clad, they look on it as an ill *Omen*; so that when any of ours did approach the *Bashaw's*, in a black Habit, they look'd a-squint on us, and made sad Complaints; and the Truth is, none of their own appear in black, but either one that is desperately poor, or else so overwhelm'd with some great Calamity, that he regards not what Cloaths he wears. A Purple Colour is a creditable Colour with them; only it is an Omen of much Bloodshed in Time of War: But the ordinary approved Colours among them, are the *White*, the *Yellow*, the *Sea-Green*, the *Violet-Colour*, and *Mouse-Colour*, &c.

THE *Turks* ascribe very much to *Augury*, and *Omens*, Good or Bad, so that it hath been known, that some *Bashaws* have been removed from their Places and Offices, by reason of a Fall from their Horse; as if that were an *Omen* of some ill Luck, which is averted from the Publick, by falling on the Head of that private and particular Person; who is thereupon degraded.

FROM *Ancyra*, we came to a Village called *Balygazar*, and from thence to *Zarekuct*; from *Zarekuct* to *Zermeczii*, and to the Bank of the River *Halys*: As we past through a Village called *Algii*, we saw, at some Distance, the neighbouring Mountains of *Synopi*, which were red, like Vermillion; and from which Red Lead is called *Synopi*.

THIS *Halys* is the famous River which was heretofore the Boundary of the two Kingdoms of the *Medes* and *Lydians*; concerning which, there was an ancient Oracle, That when *Crœsus* pass'd it to make War on the *Persians*, he should overthrow a great Empire, which fell out to be his Own; whereas he thought it would have been the *Persians*. Near the Bank of this River, there was a Wood, which seemed to us, to bear an unknown Shrub; but when we drew near, we found it to be *Liquorice*, and with the Juice of its Root, we refreshed our selves abundantly.

NEAR that River, we met with a Countryman, and asking him, by an Interpreter, Whether that River did abound with Fish? And how they used to catch them? He answered, That there were Fishes enough; but no Body could catch them. When he saw we wondred at his Answer, he proceeded: For, *says he*, if a Man strive to take them up in his Hands, away presently they swim, and will not stay to be catched. This Answer was the less surprizing to me, because, when we had lighted upon some unknown Birds, and demanded of the Country-men, *how we might take them?* One or other of them told us, That they could not be taken; for if any Body endeavoured to lay Hands on them, they would fly away.

BUT one of my Collegues, *Francis Hay*, having some Nets with him, caused them to be cast for the catching of Fish; we took a great Draught of them, and especially the *Silurus*, or *Sheathfish*, which are common in the *Danow*. Besides, there is in that River, good Store of Sea-Crabs, or else, a Sort of Fish very like them. Whereupon, the *Turks*, who saw our Fishing, wondered at the Industry and Ingenuity of *Christians*, who would catch Fish at that Rate. Hereupon, perhaps, you will say, What, are there no Fishermen in *Turkey*? I grant there are; but very few of them live in those Parts. And, I remember, in another Place, when the *Turks* saw us turn the Stream out of its Course to catch Gudgeons at the Bottom, they laughed much at us. *What*, said they, *do you catch such small guddling Fish? what are they good for?* This Ninny-Hammer did not understand, that a great many of those Fishes would make a dainty Dish, enough to suffice many Guests. But the *Turks* are so parsimonious, that they don't study their Bellies at all; give them but Bread and Garlic, or an Onion, with a Sort of *Bonniclabber*, or sour Milk, known in *Galen*'s Time, by the Name of

Syllabub, but called by them, *Ingurthe*; they feed like Farmers, and desire nothing more.

They make this Drink thus; they dilute this Milk with cold Water, and then cram Bread into it. This they use in the hottest Weather, and when they are more athirst; and we our selves found great Benefit by it, in our greatest Droughts. It is a Repast very grateful to the Palate and Stomach, and of admirable Vertue in quenching the most vehement Thirst: There is abundance of it ready made for Sale in all the *Turkish* Inns, or *Caravasera's*, as well as all other Sorts of Soop. As for hot Meat, or Flesh, the *Turks* don't much use them in their Travels; their usual Dyet, on the Road, are *Syllabubs, Cheese, dry'd Plumbs, Pears, Peaches, Quinces, Figs, Raisins*, and *Cornel-berries*; all these are exposed to sale in great earthen Platters boiled in clean Water; every one takes what he likes best. Those Fruits, with Bread, is his Food; and the Water which remains, serves for Drink. Thus their Meat and Drink stand them in very little; so that I dare say, one *Christian* spends more Money, on his Belly, in one Day, than a *Turk* doth in twelve; yea, their most solemn Feasts consist of *Wafers, Cakes*, and such-like Junkets, together with several Dishes of *Rice*, with some *Mutton*, and *Pullet*; for *Capons* are not yet known in *Turkey*; but as for *Pheasants, Thrushes*, and Birds called *Figeaters*, they never so much as heard of their Names. But, if *Honey* and *Sugar* be mix'd with the Water, the Drink is like *Jove's Nectar* to them. One Sort of their Liquors I had almost forgot, 'tis this. They take *Raisins of the Sun*, and bruise, or grind them in a Mill, and then put them into a wooden Vessel, pouring a certain Proportion of hot Water upon them. This Mixture they stir about a little, and then cover the Vessel close, and suffer it to ferment a Day or two; if it works well, then they add Lees of Wine to quicken the Operation. When it first begins to ferment, if you taste it, 'tis over-sweet, and that makes it more unpalatable; but afterwards it acquires something of an Acid Taste, which, mix'd with the Sweet, is very grateful to the Palate for about three or four Days; especially if it be mixed with Snow, of which there is plenty at *Constantinople* at all times. This Drink they call *Arabsorbet*, i. e. the *Arabian Potion*. It will not keep long, but grows sour in a very little Time. 'Twill fly up in your Head, and make you reel as bad as any Wine, if you drink too much of it; and therefore, the *Turks*, by the rules of their Religion, are forbidden to drink it. For my Part, I liked it very well; yea, that sort of Grapes was very acceptable and refreshing; in many Places they keep them all Summer long. The way of preserving them, they told me, was this: They take large Bunches of Grapes ston'd (as the hot Sun quickly ripens them in those Countries); these they put into a Wooden or Earthen Vessel, in the Bottom whereof, they first lay a Line of groun'd Mustard-Seed; then they spread a Line of Grapes upon it; thus with a Lay of Grapes, and a Lay of grinded Mustard-Seed, they fill it up to the Top; and, when the Vessel is full, then they pour in new *Must*, as much as will fill all the Interstice; then they shut it close, and so let it stand till the hot Time of the next Year, when Men stand most in need of Drink. Then these Vessels are broach'd, and the Grapes, with its Liquor, are set to sale. The *Turks* like the Liquor as well as the Grapes; but I did not so well like the Taste of the Mustard-Seed, and, therefore, I caused the Grapes to be washed, and then, when I was most thirsty, they gave me great Relief. I hope you will give me leave to commend a Food to you, that did me so much good, seeing the *Egyptians* esteemed their Herbs and Plants, which were contributory to their Health, as so many *Deities*. But 'tis Time for a Wanderer to return back into the Way.

From the Bank of the River *Halys*, which the *Turks* call *Aitoczu*, we came to *Gonkurthoy*; from thence to *Choron*, and from thence to *Theke Thioi*, where the *Turks* have a stately Monastry for their *Priests* and *Monks*, called *Dervises*. Those *Dervises* told us a great Story of a certain Man, called *Chederles*, of an huge Stature, and graveness of Mind answerable thereto. They suppose it was the same with our St. *George*, and ascribe the same Exploits to him; as the saving of a Virgin by the Slaughter of a huge and terrible *Dragon*. To which they add many Fables and Imaginations of idle Brains; as that he travelled over several Countries far and near, and at last came to a River, whose Waters made those that drank them immortal; but in what Part of the World this River is, they cannot tell us; they say, moreover, that it lies somewhere in a great Cloud, or Mist of Darkness, and that never a Man saw it since *Chederles*. As for *Chederles* himself, he was made Immortal, and so was his Horse, by drinking the same Water, who now, both do invisibly travel over the World, delighting in Wars, and appearing therein to the most Valiant, or to those who implore his Aid, of what Religion soever they be: Such ridiculous Fancies do they please themselves with! To which we may add, other Things as absurd as those before-mentioned, That he was one of the Friends and Companions of *Alexander the Great*. For, the Truth is, the *Turks* keep no just Account either of Times or Ages, but makes a confused Hodge-podge of all History. When they have a Mind to it, they scruple not to say, *That* Job *was Master of the Horse to King* Solomon, *and that* Alexander the Great *was General of his Army*; with such-like Stuff.

In that Monastry, or Mosque, there is a Fountain that bubbles forth very clear and limpid Water; it is built about and cover'd with most excellent Marble, and they ridiculously would have People believe, that it had its Original from *Chederles*'s Horses, which he pissed in great Plenty in that Place. They also told us many *Rodomontado*'s concerning the Companions of *Chederles*, concerning his chief Groom, and also concerning his Nephew by his Sister, all which were buried near at hand, and their Sepulchres there to be seen; and when any Suppliants come to pay their Devotions to them, they would have persuaded us, that they receive great Relief thereby; yea, they superstitiously affirm, That the Fragments of the Stones, and the very Earth itself, on which *Chederles*'s Feet stood, when he staid for the Dragon, if drank in any Liquor, are very good against Fevers, the Head-Ach, and the

Diseases of the Eyes. All the Country thereabout, is full of Dragons and Vipers, so that, in the hot Season of the Year, they are so thick, basking themselves in the Sun, that the Ways are almost unpassable for Travellers.

I had almost forgot to tell you, that, whereas, the *Greeks* do usually paint St. *George* on Horseback in their Temples, with his Squire behind him, holding out to him a Cup of Wine as to his Master, he being (as they believe) their *Chederles*; they laugh heartily at that Spectacle.

At this Place, we were near our Journey's End, for now we had but one Stage more to *Amasia*; and that was *Baglison*; from thence we reached *Amasia, April 7*, and thirty Days after, we left *Constantinople*. As we were coming, some *Turks* met us, to gratulate our Arrival, and to introduce us with Honour.

Amasia is, in a manner, the chief City of *Cappadocia*, where the *Turkish* Governor of that Province usually had his Residence, for the Administration of Justice, and where he usually forms his Camp. But that Town, ever since *Bajazet*'s Time, seemed to be very unlucky, and of late, the miserable Case of *Mustapha* hath confirmed it to be an unfortunate Seat. *Strabo* writes, that he was born there. It lies on the Side of two opposite Hills, the River *Iris* dividing the City of the midst, running between them; so that from each Part you may look down upon the River, as from the Seats or Stairs of a Theatre; and one Side of it is conspicuous and open to the view of the other. It is so encompassed with Hills, that there is but one way to it, either for Coach or Waggon.

The same Night we came thither, there happened a great Fire, which the *Janizaries* quenched, as their manner is, by plucking down the Houses adjoining. Upon occasion of this Accident, give me leave to inform you, that the *Turkish* Soldiers are well-pleased when a Fire happens; for, whereas they must be employed to quench it, and usually do it by ruining the contiguous Houses, they have thereby an opportunity to rifle and plunder both; so that they themselves do oftentimes privily set Houses on Fire, that so they may filch and steal what they can out of them; as I remember once, when I was at *Constantinople*, there were frequent Conflagrations of Houses. 'Twas plain, they could not happen casually, but must be set on Fire a purpose, and yet the Authors could not be found; but the Fault was commonly cast on some *Persian* Spies that were in Town: At last, upon a diligent Search, 'twas found that the Soldiers had stirr'd up their Fellows, that were a Ship-board, to do the Feat; that so, during the Fire, they might enrich themselves with the Spoils.

Upon an high Hill, that hangs over and commands *Amasia*, there is a strong Castle, wherein the *Turks* have a continual Garrison, either to curb the *Asiaticks*, who are not very well pleased with the *Ottoman* Yoke (as I shall shew anon) or else to bridle the *Persian*, who many times make large Excursions even as far as this Town, though at such a vast distance from them. In this Hill there are some ancient Monuments, which, perhaps, were the Sepulchres of the *Cappadocian* Kings.

As for the Houses and Streets of *Amasia*, there is little or no Beauty in them. Their Houses are built of Loom, as they are in *Spain*, plain at top without any Roof, and what covering they have is of Loom or Clay too. They have some old piece of a Pillar, Cylinder or Roller, which they turn up and down to stop any Chink or Crevice, made either by Rain or Wind. The Inhabitants, in former Times, lay down to sleep in the open Air. As for Rains, they are not great, nor frequent in those Parts; but if at any time a Shower falls, the Loomy Droppings from the Eaves, do wofully dirty the Cloths of those that pass under them. I saw there a certain young noble Person, living not far from me, at his Supper, after the old *Roman* fashion, lying on a Bed. As soon as I came to *Amasia*, we were introduced to compliment the supreme Vizier *Achmet*, and the rest of the *Bashaw*'s, for their Emperor was then gone abroad; we treated with them a while concerning the Contents of our Embassy; and because they would not seem to prejudice us, they lent us a favourable Ear; referring all, however, to the Will and Pleasure of their Emperor. When he came home, we were led into his Presence, for Audience; but he entertain'd us (and the Reasons we alledg'd in the Speech we made him, according to the Command of my Master) with a sour and frowning Look. He sate upon a low Throne, not above a Foot from the Ground, but it was all covered over with rich Tapestry, and with Cushions exquisitely wrought. His Bow and Arrows lay by his side, he himself (as I said) looked sternly upon us; and yet there was a certain Majesty, mix'd with Severity, in his Countenance. Each of us, as we entred the Room, was led up towards him by some of his Bed-chamber Officers, who held us by the Arm, (for so they use to introduce Ambassadors, ever since a certain *Croatian*, desiring to speak with

Amurath, and drawing near to him so to do, slew him in revenge of the death of his Master, *Mark* the *Despot* of *Servia*, who was killed by the said *Amurath*): and afterwards, as if we had kiss'd his Hand, we were led backward to the opposite part of the Room; for the *Turks* count it an unmannerly thing to turn any of their Back-parts to their Prince. From thence I had liberty to declare our Master's Commands; but they suited not with his lofty, imperious Spirit, who thought that nothing ought to be denied him, for they were daring and high; so that he, as disdaining them, said nothing but *Giusel, Giusel!* (i. e.) *Well, Well!* And so we were dismissed to our Lodgings.

At our Audience there was a very full Court, for a great many Governors of Provinces were there with their Presents; and, besides the Imperial Horse, *Spahi's*, *Janipagits* and *Ululags*, there were also a great number of *Janizaries*. But, among this vast number of Courtiers, there was not so much as one more eminent for Birth and Parentage; each one, by his Valour and adventurous Atchievements, was the Carver out of his own Fortune. Their Honour ariseth from their Preferments; so that there is no dispute about Precedency, but every Man's Pre-eminces is according to the Office which he bears. And those Offices are distributed at the meer Will and Pleasure of the Prince, who does not regard the empty Name of Nobility, nor value a Rush the Favour of the Multitude, or of any other particular Man; but, considering only the Merits and Disposition of the Man, he rewards him accordingly. And, by that means, Employments are bestowed upon such Persons as are best able to manage them; and every Man hath an opportunity to be the Hammerer out of his own Honour and Preferment. Those which at present are the greatest Officers under their Emperor, were mostly the Sons of Shepherds or Neatherds; and they are so far from being ashamed of the Meanness of their Original, that they glory therein among one another; and account it more Praise-worthy to be the Advancers of themselves, than if they had Honour transmitted down to them from their Ancestors.

For thus they argue, Virtue is not propagated from our Parents, but is partly the Gift of God, and partly acquired by good Discipline, and by our own Labour and Industry; so that, as no Son hath his Father's Skill in Music, Arithmetic or Geometry, derived to him from his Birth, so neither can Fathers bequeath Virtue as an Inheritance to their Children; for the

Soul, say they, is not communicated with the Father's Seed (so that a Son must necessarily be born alike qualified as his Father was) but it is infus'd into his Body from the God of Heaven. Thus in that Nation, Dignities, Honours, Offices, *&c.* are the Rewards of Virtue and Merit; as on the other side, Dishonesty, Sloth, and Idleness, are among them the most despicable things in the whole World. And by this means they flourish, bear sway, and enlarge the Bounds of their Empire every day more and more. But we, *Christians*, to our shame be it spoken, live at another manner of rate; Virtue is little esteemed among us, but Nobleness of Birth (forsooth) carries away all the Honour and Preferment. But enough of this at present: More may be spoken on this Argument hereafter; and what I have now said about it, pray keep it to your self, for other Men may not be able to bear my Freedom herein.

To return, then, to my Subject; I shall now present you with a surprizing Spectacle, even a multitude of Persons with picket Turbants on their Heads, made of pure white Linnen folded together in Plates; their other Apparel was very costly, of several Sorts and Colours, all most radiantly shining with Gold, Silver, Purple, Silk, Velvet, *&c.* I am not able to describe the Gaudiness of the *Show*; in one Word, 'twas the most glorious one I ever saw in all my Life. And yet, in all this Splendor, there was a great deal of Simplicity and Parsimony too. Those who were of one Order had Cloathing all of one sort; there were no foolish Hems, Lacings, Fringes or Borders, as among us, which cost a great deal of Money, and yet wear out in a day or two. The Silk and Velvet Suits, which many of them wore, though mightily embroidered, yet cost not above a Ducat the making and embroidering. They did as much admire to see the Fashion of our Cloaths, as we did that of theirs. Their Vests are very long, almost down to their Heels, which is more graceful, and makes them seem taller than they are; but our Apparel (forsooth) is so curtail'd and short, that it hardly covers the Parts which Nature would have to be concealed; on which Account it is less decent. Besides, it seems to take away some Inches from the Tallness of our Stature, and look more *Dwarf-like.* And yet, among so great a Multitude, I took notice of this most laudable Circumstance; 'twas all *hush*; not so much as a word spoken among them all, nor no humming Noise, as among a tumultuous Multitude; no justling one of another, but every particular Man quietly kept his own Station. The Heads of them, which they call *Aga's*, had Seats to sit upon, such as their *Serasquiers*, or *Generals*, their *Brigadiers*,

Colonels and *Captains*; but the Commonalty stood on their Feet. Among the rest, I most admir'd the *Janizaries*; though there were some Thousands of them, yet they stood at a distance one from another; Stock-still, (as we say) as if they had been Statues: So that I, who was at some distance from them, thought verily they had been so, till being advised to salute them, as the manner is, I saw them all bow their Heads, by way of Resalutation, unto me. When we passed from this Shew, behold there was another pleasurable one, which entertain'd us; and that was their Horse-Guards, in their March to their Quarters. They rode upon gallant stately Prancers, excellently well trapped, equipped, and Shod. Thus we were dismissed, but with little hopes of obtaining what we came for.

On the 10th of *May*, the *Persian* Ambassador came to *Amasia*, and brought with him rich and gallant Presents, as many choice sorts of Hangings, *Babylonian* Tents, curiously wrought within with many sorts of Needle-work, gallant Horse-Trappings, and Saddles, Scymiters made at *Damascus*, whose Handles were studded with Jewels, and Shields of curious Workmanship; but that which exceeded them all, was the *Alcoran*, so they call the Book containing the Rites and Ceremonies of their Religion, which they fancy *Mahomet* compos'd by Divine Inspiration, and which is accounted the most noble Present of all. They quickly accorded with him on Terms of Peace, so that it concern'd us to be cautious, who were to find greater obstruction in our Negotiations with them. And, to assure us that the Peace was confirm'd betwixt them, they omitted no manner of extraordinary Respect to their Ambassador. For the manner of the *Turks* is, (as I told you before,) to be excessive on both Sides, either in bestowing Honour on their Friends, or in heaping Reproaches on their Enemies. *Haly Basha*, Deputy to the *Grand Vizier*, treated the *Persian* with a sumptuous Dinner, which he made in his Garden, a Place far distant from us, and separated also by the interposal of the River, yet we could see the Manner of it well enough; for, I told you, the Place was seated so high on both sides of the Hill, that the Eye might easily discover what was done on each side. This *Haly* is a *Dalmatian* by Birth, a Man of much Wit, and, which is strange in *Turkey*, very courteous to Strangers. The Table, at which the *Bashaw* and the *Persian* Embassador sate, was covered over with a Canopy, and the Dishes were served up after this manner. There were one hundred Youths, which attended, like Waiters, all of them alike habited. First of all, they entered one by one, at a small distance from each other, till the Train of them reached up to the Table where the Guests were sitting. They had nothing at all in their Hands, that so they might not be hindered in saluting the Guests, which was done in this manner; they laid their Hands on their Thighs, and bowed their Heads downwards to the Ground; when this Ceremony was perform'd, then he that stood next the Kitchen, took a Dish and gave it to the next Page immediately before him; he handed it to a Third, and he to a Fourth, and so from one to another till it came to him who stood next the Table, and he delivered it to the Hands of the Gentleman-Sewer, who plac'd it on the Table. And thus one hundred Dishes, or more, were serv'd up to the Table in excellent Order, without any Noise at all; and, when that was done, those Waiters, or Pages, saluted the Guests a second time, and so returned in the same Order they came in; only, of course, those that were last before went out first, and those which were nearest the Table brought up the Rear. Thus the second Course was also serv'd up; so that the *Turks* are great Admirers of Orders, even in the smallest matters, which we *Christians* are apt to neglect, even in things of greatest Moment. At some distant from the Ambassador sate his Attendants with some *Turks* of Quality with them.

PEACE being thus made with the *Persians*, as I told you before, yet we could get no good Terms of them at all, only we obtain'd an half year's Truce, till I could send to my Master, and know his Answer. I was sent to be *Leiger* Ambassador there; but, in regard there was no Peace settl'd betwixt both Empires, the *Bashaws* thought it adviseable for me to return to my Master with Letters from *Solyman* their Emperor; and I was to return with an Answer from his Imperial Majesty, if he thought fit. Hereupon I was again introduced into *Solyman*'s Presence, and had two large embroider'd Veils, reaching down to my Ancles, clap'd upon me; they were so heavy, that I could hardly stand under them. My Family also, that attended me, were all clad with silk Garments of divers Colours; in this Posture I stalked along, like *Agamemnon*, or some such piece of Gravity, in a *Tragedy*; and so I took my leave of their Emperor, having first receiv'd Letters from him to my Master, seal'd and wrap'd up in Cloth of Gold, and the chief of my Attendants were also admitted to take their Leaves; and thus, after we had taken our leaves of the *Bashaws*, I and my Collegues departed from *Amasia*, *June* the 2d. The Custom is, that Ambassadors at their Departure, have a Dinner provided for them in the *Divan*, (so they call the place where the *Bashaws* sit to administer Justice,) but this is done only to their Friends;

that Compliment was omitted to me, because Affairs were not yet in an amicable Posture between them and us.

IF you ask me, what manner of Man *Solyman* was, I'll tell you. He was an ancient Man, his Countenance, and the Mien of his Body, were very majestick, well becoming the Dignity which he bore; he was frugal and temperate, even from his Youth, though he might have taken a greater Liberty to himself by the Rules of their own Religion. In his younger Days he was not given to Wine, nor to masculine Venery, which the *Turks* much delight in; to that his very Enemies could object nothing against him on those Accounts, but that he was too uxurious, and his over-indulgence to his Wife made him give way to the Death of his Son *Mustapha*: Yet that Crime was vulgarly imputed to an Ascendent she had over him, by reason of her Inchantments and Love-Portions. This is certain, that, after he once took her for his lawful Wife, he never had carnal Knowledge of any other Woman, though their Laws did not forbid him. He is a very strict Observer of the *Mahumetan* Religion, and is as desirous to propagate that, as to enlarge the Bounds of his Empire.

HE is now sixty years of Age; and, for a Man of his Years, he enjoys a moderate proportion of Health, and yet his Countenance doth discover, that he carries about him some hidden Disease, 'tis thought a Gangrene, or Ulcer, in the Thigh; yet at solemn Audiences of Ambassadors, he hath a *Fucus* to paint his Cheeks with, that he may appear sound and healthy to them, and thereupon be more dreaded by foreign Princes, their Masters. Methought, I discovered some such thing at my Dismission; for his Countenance was as sour when I left him, as it was at my first Audience.

HAVING thus taken my leave, I began my Journey in the Month of *June*, and the Heat thereof was so excessive, that it cast me into a Fever. 'Tis true, it was a remiss and gentle one, yet it came every Day; to which was added an Hoarseness, and Defluction of Rheum from the Head, and it held me till I came to *Constantinople*.

THE *Persian* Embassador left *Amasia* the self-same Day that I did, and we went both out of the City the same way; for, (as I told you before) there is but one Passage into, or out of, that Town, it is so shut in by the circumjacent and unpassable Hills: But the Way quickly doth divide into two, one to the *East*, which the *Persians* took; and another to the *West*.

which was our Road. In the open Fields about the Town, we saw the *Turkish* Camp pitch'd, with abundance of Tents. I shall not entertain you with the Stages of my Return, they being the same with those of my Journey thither, only we made a little more Speed, and sometimes rode two Day's Journey in one. In fine, we came to *Constantinople, June* the 2d. You must needs think I had a troublesome Journey of it, having such a Companion with me, as a *Quotidian Ague,* all the way; so that, when I came thither, I was almost nothing but Skin and Bone: Yet, lean as I was, when I came to rest, and by the advice of *Quaquelben,* my Physician, used warm Baths, I quickly recovered. One thing I observed in the method of my Cure, that, when I came out of the warm Bath, he would sprinkle me over with cold Water, which, though it were troublesome to me at the present, yet I found that it did me much good.

Whilst I staid at *Constantinople,* there was a certain Person, that came from the *Turkish* Camp in *Asia,* who told me a Story, which I shall acquaint you with, because it shows that the *Asiaticks* are not very well pleased, either with the Religion, or the Government of the *Turks.* 'Twas this: *Solyman,* says he, as he was returning home, was forc'd to lodge one Night in the House of a certain *Asiatick,* and when he went away in the Morning, his Host brought a great deal of Perfume, and us'd a great many Ceremonies, to cleanse and purge his House, as if it had been polluted by such a Guest as *Solyman;* when *Solyman* heard of it, he caused the Man to be slain, and his House to be levelled with the Ground. This Punishment the poor Man underwent for his Aversion to the *Turks,* and his Propensity to favour the *Persians.*

I staid about fourteen Days at *Constantinople* to refresh my self, and then I entred on my Journey back again to *Vienna*: But I was entertain'd with an inauspicious Omen, even a very sad Spectacle; just as I was gone out of the Gates of *Constantinople,* I met whole Waggon-Loads of Boys and Girls, which were brought out of *Hungary* to *Constantinople* to be sold; no Merchandize is more frequent amongst them than that. For, as when we leave *Antwerp,* we meet with all sorts of merchantable Commodities importing into the Town, so here, ever now and then, there passed by us abundance of poor miserable *Christian* Slaves, which were going to be sold in the Markets to a perpetual Bondage. There was no distinction of Age; Old and Young were driven in Herds, or Companies, or else were tied in a long Chain, as we use to tail Horses when we carry them to Fairs. When I beheld this woful sight, I could not forbear weeping and bemoaning the unhappy State of poor *Christendom*. And if that miserable Spectacle were not afflicting enough to a new Traveller, take another bad and mortifying Occurrence: My Collegues had recommended some of their Retinue to me, which were weary of living in *Turkey*, that they might be of my Train, in returning to their own Country. I granted their Request, and having travelled two Day's Journey, I perceiv'd one that was Chief among them, (called a *Vaivode*, from his Office,) was carried sick in a Coach; one of his Feet being bare, without any Stockings, he would not suffer it to be covered, for he had in it a Plague-sore, which he found more easy to keep open. We were much troubled at this sight, as fearing that infectious Disease would spread farther; but the poor Man liv'd till we came to *Adrianople*, and there departed this Life. Upon his Death another Mischief did succeed; as soon as the Breath was out of his Body, the rest of the *Hungarians* ran in greedily to the Prey, one caught up his Stockings, another his Doublet, a third his Shirt, a fourth his other Linnen; thus casting themselves, and us too, into a great deal of Danger. Nor was there any way in the World to hinder them.

'Tis true, my Physician, like an honest Man, ran in amongst them, and intreated them, for God's sake, to throw the Things away, because they would infect us all; but they were deaf to his Advice. The Day after we left *Adrianople*, those very Persons came to him, and complain'd of a Pain in their Heads, with a dejection of their Spirits, and a Listlessness both of Body and Mind, and desired his Advice; he, suspecting the Symptoms of the Plague in the case, told them, they were well enough serv'd, for not harkening to his Counsel; yet he would do them what good he could, only, being on his Journey, he was unprovided of proper Medicines. The same Day I walked abroad into the Field, as I us'd to do, as soon as ever I came to my Inn, to see if I could find any thing worthy of my Notice in those Countries, where I met with an unknown Herb in the Meadow, which smelt like *Garlick*. After I had pluck'd some Leaves of it, I gave them to my Physician to know his Judgment; he looked wistly upon it, and told me, 'twas *Scordium*, and lifting up his Hands to Heaven, he gave God thanks for sending us so opportune a Remedy against the Plague; hereupon he gathers a great quantity of it, and putting it into a large Pot, boiled it over the Fire. Then he bid the *Hungarians* take heart, and parted the Decoction amongst them, prescribing the taking of it very hot, as they were going to Bed, mix'd with some *Lemnian* Earth, and *Diascordium*, and that they should not sleep till they had fallen into a great Sweat. Observing his Directions, the next Day after they were much better, and desired the same Portion again, and when they had drunk it, they grew perfectly well. And thus, by God's Blessing, we avoided that Infection.

AND yet, the residue of our Journey was not without Peril. After we had passed the Country of the *Thracians* and *Bulgarians*, which reaches as far as *Nissa*, and came into the *Servians* Country, reaching from *Nissa* to *Simandria*, where the *Rascians* Country begins; we came at last to *Belgrade*, the Weather being excessively hot and parching, for 'twas the hottest time of the *Dog-days*.

AT *Belgrade*, upon one of our Fish-days, we were presented with abundance of choice Fish, and amongst the rest, with large full-bodied *Carps*, taken in the *Danube*, whose *Carps* are very much commended: My People did eat very greedily of them, and that was either the cause, or the occasion, which cast many of them into a Fever; yet all that quantity of Fish, which was enough to satisfy forty Men, cost but half a Dollar; and the Truth is, other Things are as cheap. As for Hay, 'tis little or nothing worth; the Meadows are so laden with it, that every Man may take what he will, provided he pay for the Mowing and Carriage; which made us admire the Wisdom of the old *Hungarians*, after they had passed the *Save*, who chose so fertile a Country, as *Hungary*, to dwell in; where there were all manner of Conveniences for Human Life. We passed over a great Tract of Land, both beyond and on this side the *Save*, and we found the Grass, Barley, Oats and Wheat, almost parch'd and withered with Drought; but as soon as we entred *Hungary*, the Grass was so tall, that a Coach, that went before, could hardly be seen by another that came after; which is a great Argument of the goodness of the Soil.

THE *Rascians*, as I told you before, begin at *Simandria*, and reach as far as the River *Drave*; they are reputed to be a fudling sort of People, and not very faithful to Strangers. Whence they had their Name and Original, I do not certainly know; but truly they were kind enough to us; we passed through some Villages of theirs of less Note, and at last arrived at *Esseck*, which is almost inclosed with muddy Marshes, and is famous for the slaughter of *Catzianerus*, and the overthrow of the *Christians*. Here I was taken with a *Tertian Ague*, I was so parch'd with Heat, in travelling the open Fields of *Hungary*; and at *Esseck* we passed the *Drave*, and came to *Lasque*, where being weary with the Heat of my Journey, and my Ague, I laid me down to Rest. There the chiefest of the Place came to me to bid me welcome; and presented me with large Melons, Pears, and Plumbs of several Sorts, besides Wine, and other Provisions, all of them very good; the noted Country of *Campania* in *Italy* hardly bears better. In the Room where I lodged, there was a long Table all furnished with these Viands: My Servants desired the *Hungarians* to stay to Supper, excusing my Absence, because of my Sickness. As soon as I awoke, and saw such a full-spread Table before my Eyes, I thought verily I had been in a Dream, and ask'd my Physician, how that came about? He told me plainly, that he himself had caused the Table to be furnished, that so the very Sight of it might refresh me. But must I not taste of it, said I? Yes, said he, but you must only taste; and so I eat a little of it, and seem'd to be much the better for it. The Day after the *Hungarians* came to me again to present their Service, desiring me to represent their Condition to the Emperor, in regard of the Wrongs they received from some of their Neighbours. From thence we came to *Mohatz*, noted for the Overthrow and Death of *Lewis* King of *Hungary*; not far from that Town, I saw a River whose Water was deep, and its Banks very steep; here that unhappy Prince leapt in with his Horse, and was drown'd, being for his Fall as much to be lamented, as for his Imprudence, in venturing with a small and newly rais'd Army of his Country-Men, to cope with the more numerous, veteran, and well-disciplin'd Forces of *Solyman*.

From *Mohatz*, we travelled on to *Tulna*, and from thence to *Felduar*. There I passed over the *Danube*, into an Island, pretty large, called *Cophis*, inhabited by *Rascians*; and so repassing the *Danube*, I arrived at *Buda* twelve Days after I left *Belgrade*, *August* the 4th, having lost many of my Horses by the way, who were choaked with eating new Barley, and drinking over-cold Water. Besides, I narrowly escaped Robbers, which these Countries are much infested with, especially by those they call *Heydukes*, some of which were afterwards taken, and put to death at *Buda*, where they confessed to the *Bashaw* thereof, that they lay in wait for me and my Train, under a broken Bridge we were to pass, that so they might assault us unawares. The Truth is, a few may very easily circumvent and destroy a great many Passengers on such Bridges; for the Bridges are ill-built, and the Planks are set so wide, and gaping one from another, that you can scarce go over them safe on Horseback, without danger of falling, if you are never so careful; and if some meet you before, others will fall on your Rear, and others start out from the Reeds and Sedges below, where they hide themselves, and so accost you in the Flank, and you can hardly manage your Horse for Self-defence, by reason of the badness of the Bridge: No doubt you may be treated as the *Romans* were in the *Caudine Streights*; be either taken, or killed, at Pleasure. I know not what it was that deterred them from assaulting us; whether it were our Numbers, or the Sight of the *Hungarians* with us; or because we were in a long Train, and all were not on the Bridge at once; or whatever else it was that withheld them, by God's Blessing, we got safe to *Buda*. The *Bashaw* of the Town was not then at home; he was gone to *Pest*, on the other side of the River, where they had a Council of War, after the manner of the *Hungarians*, they call them *Rachi*. Many *Sanziacks* were already come thither, but more were expected; for which Cause, when I desired Audience, 'twas put off for three Days, that the *Janizaries* and military Persons might make a greater Show. Then I was sent for over, and conveyed to his Tent, where he made Complaints to me of the Injuries that some *Hungarians* had done him. It is usual, in those frontier Garrisons, both for *Hungarians* and *Turks*, mutually to complain of one another; yea, sometimes they, that are most in Fault, begin to complain first. The *Turkish* Bashaw also added some threatning Expressions of Revenge. It may be, he thought that the Sight of his Army would terrify me; but he was mistaken. I answered him roundly, that the *Hungarians* might rather find Fault with the *Turks*, than on the contrary; for I my self, in my Travels, had seen some of his Soldiers plunder some *Hungarians*, Subjects of his Imperial Majesty, and carry away their Goods. He answered me, he had indeed put some contumacious *Christians* under military Execution; but they were such as were under his Master, not the Emperor. Thus, after a mutual Altercation, I was dismissed, being in very bad plight, for my Ague-Fit was strong upon me all that Day.

THE Day after, I went to *Gran*, having a *Turkish* Guard of Horse along with me. I had a mind to be wafted over the *Danube*, and for one Night to lodge in a Village over against the Castle of *Gran*, that the Day after I might come the sooner to *Commara*, and be better able to endure my Ague-Fit, which I expected that Day; and therefore I entreated that Favour of my Guide, that he would send some body over, to bring the Ferry-Boat, that was on the other Side, that so our Passage might be the easier. I found some Difficulty in having my Request granted; yet, partly to gratify me, and partly to acquaint the *Sanziacks* with my Arrival there, he sent over two Persons. When they were gone an Hour before, they spied four Horsemen standing under a Tree, a little from the High-way-side. They judged them, by their Habits, to be *Turks*, and therefore turned aside to accost them; and, as they drew near, they ask'd them, What News? They answered not a Word; but made at them with their drawn Swords, and gave one of them such a Blow, athwart his Face, that he made the greatest Part of his Nose to hang down over his Chin; and then catching at his Horse, which he held by the Bridle, he left his own Beast, and mounting it, set Spurs, and away. The *Turks* presently came back to us, especially he with the maim'd Face, and, with a woful Lamentation, bid us prepare for the Combat, for we were Way-laid. I, to encourage my Men, got presently on Horse-back; but we came too late, when the Scuffle was over; for they had more mind to preserve the Prey they had got, than to fight; and thereupon fled speedily to *Javarin*, a Garrison of ours, to which they did belong: The *Turks* shewed them to us, as they were scouring over the neighbouring Hills that led to *Javarin*. Thus we came to *Gran*; the *Sanziack* very friendly gave me a Visit, and, among other Discourse, he put me in mind of the Insolency of the *Hungarian* Soldiers, who could not be kept from Thieving (said he) though you, the Emperor's Ambassador, were in company of those they robbed; and therefore he desired of me, that the Horse they took away yesterday might be restored. In the mean Time, the *Turk*, that was wounded the Day before, stood without in the Entry, with his Nose sewed together, through which he made a lamentable Moan, desiring me to pity his Condition. I told him, I would give him what was enough for his Cure, and so I bestowed two Duckets upon him. He would have had more; but the *Sanziack* told him, 'twas enough; his Misfortune was not to be charged upon me.

BEING thus dismissed by the *Sanziack*, I came the same Day to *Commara*, where I expected my Ague-Fit; but when the usual Period of it drew near, I found it had left me, as if a Fever, got in *Turkey*, durst not accompany me into the *Christian* Territories. Hereupon I gave God thanks, who had both freed me of my Ague, and had also brought me safe to the end of my long and tedious Journey.

TWO Days after, I came to *Vienna*, where the Emperor *Ferdinand*, my most gracious Master, was not at present, only I found *Maximilian*, King of *Bohemia*, there in his Room; whole courteous Reception of me made me almost forget the Toil of my Journey. But I must tell you, I was so emaciated with my Sickness, and the Inconveniences of my Journey together, that many thought the *Turks* had given me a poisonous Dose; for, truly, when I went lately to pay my Duty to the Arch-Duke *Ferdinand*, he asked one of his Domesticks, who I was? who answered, I was one that came lately from *Turkey*, and that it was no wonder I looked so ill, for they, who returned from those Parts, usually did so.

PERHAPS he was willing to have it believed, that I had taken the Emperor *Claudius*'s Dose; but, for my part, I know of no such thing; neither do I question, but after resting a while, to recover the tediousness of my Journey, I shall look as well as ever I did: I find my self something mended already.

IN the mean time, I acquainted the Emperor with my Return, by Letter, and of the half Year's Truce I had obtained; and the sum of my whole Negotiation; and that, when he came home from the *Diet*, I would inform him of all Particulars more punctually and distinctly.

ONE thing more I shall acquaint you with. There were many Persons who refused to accompany me to *Constantinople*, either for Fear, or I know not what other Motive, who wished they had given me any Money to go along with me, now they saw me return in safety. But what says he in *Plautus*? *If you will eat the Kernel, you must take the Pains to break the Nut*: He does himself Wrong, that thinks to reap part of the Fruit, who took no part of the Pains.

THUS, Sir, I have given you an account of my Journey, both to *Constantinople*, and also to *Amasia*. I have not dress'd up my Narrative with Flowers of Rhetoric, but have presented you with it, just as I would have related it to you by Word of Mouth. I know you will bear with the Coarseness of my Style, it being occasioned by my over-eager Desire to gratify you; nor can you well expect Elegancy from me now in my Heat and Throng of Business, which I was never Master of in my greatest Retirements. This I assure you, both for your Information and my own Content, that I am not conscious to myself of any Falshood in the whole Narration, which is the principal Ornament of such Relations as these. Thus I bid you Farewell.

Vienna, September 1st.

SIR,

I RECEIVED your Letter, wherein you acquaint me, that you have heard of my second Voyage into *Turkey*; on which Account you express your Wonderment, that I would venture to visit that uncouth and barbarous Country, once more. And withal, you desire to know the Issue of my Journey: How I found Matters at my Return to *Constantinople*; what Entertainment I met with there; what proportion of Health I enjoy; whether my Life be pleasant to me, or not; and, in fine, what Hopes there may be of my speedy return to *Germany*. To all which you oblige me, upon the score of our ancient Friendship, to give particular and express Answers; which, to gratify you, I shall accordingly do.

KNOW then, in the first Place, that you were not mis-informed as to my Return into *Turkey*; the thing is most true: Neither could I avoid the Journey, as being oblig'd thereunto by Promise; and you know every honest Man is as good as his Word. My Case was this: The Emperor *Ferdinand*, my most gracious Lord and Master, designed me as his Lieger Ambassador to *Constantinople*; but his Design was grounded on this Supposition, that a Peace would be first settled betwixt the two Empires. Articles of Agreement, however, being not yet fully accorded to, nor wholly rejected, there was no reason I should slip my Neck out of the Collar, till the Matter was brought to some certain Issue; either a firm Peace, or a perfect Rupture. And therefore, when I foresaw what a Bushel of Troubles I should run my self into, by my Return, I had much rather a fitter Person had been substituted for the Employment; but no body being willing to accept the Charge, I was, in a manner, forced into the Service; it being my Duty to comply with, and obey, the Will and Pleasure of my gracious Master: For as soon as ever he return'd from the Imperial Diet to *Vienna*, and was informed by me of my Transactions with *Solyman*, the *Ottoman* Emperor, he immediately laid his Commands upon me to prepare my self to return, and to carry back his Answer to *Solyman*'s Letters. 'Tis true, it was the depth of Winter, when I was commanded to return to *Constantinople*; and, besides, 'twas a very rainy, cold and tempestuous Season; and my Message too was so severe, that I was like to have no Thanks for my Labour. Here, perhaps, you may twit me in the Teeth, what! Twice to the same Place? To which I answer, twice, and oftner, if there be need; for commendable Enterprizes, the mere hazardous, the more Praise-worthy.

'TWAS in *November* when I left *Vienna*, to undertake my second Voyage to unhospitable *Pontus*. I will not grate your Ears with the Relation of the Enterprizes of my *second* Journey: I was too vexatious, I fear, in giving you an Account of my *first*.

IT may suffice to tell you, that I went the same Stages, in a manner, that I did at first. So then, to *Constantinople* I came, in the beginning of *January*, having lost one of my Retinue, who died of a Fever in the way. There I found my Collegues in good Health; but a mighty Change was made in the *Turkish* Affairs: *Bajazet, Solyman*'s youngest Son, had escap'd a great Danger, and was reconciled to his Father: *Achmet Bassa*, the *Grand Vizier*, had been strangled, and *Rustan*, his Predecessor, was restored to his Place of *Grand Viziership*, of whom more hereafter. But, at present, I shall acquaint you what coarse Entertainment I met with from their *Emperor*, his Bashaws, and other great Men among them. For their Bashaws (as the manner is, before they introduce an Ambassador to their Prince) being desirous to hear of me, in general, the purport of my Message; as soon as they understood, that my Master *Cæsar* would not recede a jot from his Right, but did punctually insist upon it, as just and equal, that the Transactions with the Widow of *John* late *Vaivode* of *Transylvania* and her Son (being made without Fraud, Force or Covin,) should be strictly observed, they were in a mighty Chafe: For you must know, that a long Series of happy Success, hath so elevated the Minds of this People, that they make their own Wills, forsooth, the sole Rule of all Reason, Right or Wrong. On which presumptuous Principle, they carried it very haughtily towards us; and told us the extream Danger we should run into, if we offer'd to appear before that Prince with such an imperious Message. When such menacing Words could not deter us from demanding Audience, they gave us to understand, that they would have no hand in our Admittance; for do ye think, (said they) that we are such brazen-fac'd Fellows as to bring you, with such sawcy Answers, to our King? No, said they; it will be a plain Mockery to him, which he will never take well at your Hands. Do you not know, proceeded they, that he is come back from *Persia* with a victorious Army; where, his Successes have so exalted him, that he hath put his own Son to death, as emulous of the Empire? Whereby you may guess at the severity of his Passion. He longs for, and courts, a fair Occasion to send his hardy and well-disciplin'd Army into *Hungary*, to enrich them with the Spoils of that Country, and to add the residue thereof to his Empire. And therefore, if you be wife, don't rouze a sleeping *Lyon*; for thereby you will but hasten your own Miseries, which are coming on fast enough of themselves. Such were the Harangues of the Bashaws to us; and the rest of the *Turks* were of the same Mind. The mildest Punishment they denounced against us, was, that two of us would be cast into a nasty Dungeon; and the third (which was to be my share) would have his Nose and Ears cut off, and so sent back to his Master.

AND, to strike the greater Terror into us, the *Turks*, who passed by our Lodgings, gave us many a sour Look; which was an Argument, that they intended some cruel Deportment towards us. And the truth is, from that Day forward, they used us more coarsely than ever; they kept us up close as Prisoners rather than Ambassadors: They suffer'd no body to come to us, nor permitted any of us to go forth, and the rest of their Carriage was as intolerable. Thus have they treated us these six Months past; and I know not how long they will continue these Severities; but, come what will, we submit to the Will of God, our Cause is just and honourable, and that gives us Relief against their vigorous Extremities. But leaving the Narration of our own Misfortunes, I shall answer your Desire, in giving you an Account of the Story of *Bajazet*. For the clearer Explication thereof, I must acquaint you, that *Solyman* had five Sons; the Eldest, begot by him on a Concubine, near the *Bosphorus*, was called *Mustapha*, of whose unhappy End you have heard before; but by another Wife, named *Roxolana*, he had four, *Mahomet*, *Selimus*, *Bajazet* and *Giangir*. *Mahomet* liv'd till he was married, (for the *Turks* call their Concubines, Wives) but died soon after; so that *Selimus* and *Bajazet* of this latter Venter only remain'd alive. As for *Giangir*, he came thus to his end: When News was brought to *Constantinople*, that his Half-brother *Mustapha* was put to death, the Youth, being of a timorous Mind and infirm Body (for he was crook-back'd) fell into a grievous Passion, upon the Imagination that the like Fate did hang over his own Head; for he could promise safety to himself no longer than his Father liv'd. If his Head were once laid, he that was his Successor, would certainly kill all his Brethren, as emulous of the Kingdom; not one of them would be excepted, and himself, being among the Number, must look for the same Fate. This Thought struck him into a Disease, even as if the Bow-string had been already about his Neck, which cost him his Life; so that now only *Selimus* and *Bajazet* remained. *Selimus* was the Elder, and 'twas known to all, that his Father design'd him for the Empire; but *Bajazet* was most favoured and doted upon by his Mother. Whether it were out of Commiseration to prevent his inevitable Ruin, or else out of motherly Indulgence, or whatever else the Reason was; this is certain, if her Vote could have carried it, *Bajazet* had certainly succeeded in the Empire after his Father's Death. But she must give way to his Father's Will, who was fully resolv'd, come what would, that *Selimus*, and none else, should succeed him. *Bajazet* was not ignorant thereof, and therefore he turned every Stone to stave off his impending Fate, and, if possible, to prevent his Ruin by grasping at the Throne. And his Hopes were encreased by the favour of his Mother, and of *Rustan* the *Grand Vizier*, who was thought to have espoused his Interests. Having two such Pillars to support him, he thought with himself, 'twas far more glorious to hazard his Life in contending with his Brother for the Empire, than to die obscurely by the Bow-string, as a Victim to his Cruelty.

BAJAZET having this Project in his Head, began to pick Quarrels with his Brother, and to maintain a Faction against him; neither was it long before a proper Occasion offered itself for him to begin his design'd Enterprize, of rising in Arms upon the account of *Mustapha*'s Death, and the Disgust of many thereupon. For the Truth is, *Mustapha* was so well belov'd in his Life-time, and so much lamented at his Death, that those who had placed all their Hopes of Advancement in him alone, were almost unwilling to live after him; so that they did but wait for an Opportunity to revenge his Death, or to die as he did. Others, who were conscious to themselves that they had favoured his Party, and therefore were obnoxious to the present Power, did not care what Hurley-burlies they made; ready they were for any Innovation, only they wanted a Leader. In this case, they did not well know what to do. As for *Mustapha* himself, they knew he could not be recalled from the Dead; yet it was in their power to suborn and set up a feigned *Mustapha* in his head, as if the true one had been yet alive. This Design pleased *Bajazet* (who was the contriver of the Plot) best of all, as most conducing to the accomplishment of his Purpose. Hereupon, by his Emissaries, he procures a mean Fellow, but bold and ready witted, to counterfeit himself to be *Mustapha*; and his Pretence was the more plausible, because his Stature, Physiognomy and Meen of his Body did somewhat resemble *Mustapha*'s. This Man began first, to shew himself in that part of *Thrace* which was above *Constantinople*, towards the *Danube*, *Moldavia*, and *Valachia*. This Place he thought the most opportune to raise a Party, because it was full of Horse; and that part of the *Turkish Militia* did most favour *Mustapha*. Here he starts up, as if he had fled in Post-haste from some remote Place, with a few in his Company; which he pretended were for his own Security. His Followers being asked by the Country, who he was? They answered, at first, whisperingly, that he was *Mustapha*. Hereupon they were more desirous to know the Truth; and then he was forced to declare himself, that he was *Mustapha*, indeed. Having made this prosperous Beginning, he goes on to congratulate his Safety among them, and to give God thanks. *First*, he told them, *That, when he was sent for by his angry Father, he durst not trust himself to come into his Presence; but, by his Friend's Advice, suborned one, somewhat like him, to represent his Person, that, by another Man's Hazard rather than his own, he might make Trial of his incensed Father's Inclination towards him. This Man he hired with great Promises of Reward; but as soon as he came to his Father, he was strangled at his Tent-door, before he had any opportunity to make his Defence; and his dead Body was exposed to the View of the Soldiery. At which time,* said he, *there were some few that smelt out the Project; but most part was deceived by the disguised Lineaments of the deceased Body, and thought it was he himself that was slain. As soon as I heard of this,* said he, *I saw there was no Stay for me, but I must consult my Safety by a speedy Flight. I took but few in my Company, that I might be the less taken notice of and thus passing over* Pontus *and the* Bosphoran *Country, I am,* said he, *come hither; where I promise my self much Aid from your Fidelity, and, therefore, I beseech you lend me your helping Hand; and, seeing I am oppress'd by a wretched Step-mother, be you as forward to help me in my Affliction, as you were all ready to do so in my Prosperity. For my part, I am resolved to revenge my Wrongs, and to maintain my Life by force of Arms. For what other Course, pray, can I take? I owe my Life to my Father's Mistake, who killed another Man instead of me; so that I plainly see, what Fate attends me, if ever I come into his Power. The miserable old Man is imposed on by the enchanting Passions of a Step-mother, whom he doats upon, and by the Ministry of* Rustan, *to whatsoever Attempt they please. But, thanks be to God,* said he, *I have got some Friends left to revenge my Wrongs, and to punish my Enemies. And, besides, I am not quite daunted, but have a great stock yet of Courage left; for I know that the*

Janizaries, *and most of all my Father's Court are on my side; and, then, upon hearing of my Name, I know all those who lamented me, when dead (as they thought), will joyn me, now they hear I am alive; only be you pleased to vouchsafe me a favourable Reception, and to protect me till sufficient Aid come in to me.* These were his private, and also his public Harangues, where-ever he came; and his instructed Followers ecchoed forth the same Report; yea, some Men of Note whom *Bajazet* had suborned, sung Notes to the same Tune. Thus a great party of Men, unknown to *Bajazet*, were brought into the Noose. For the Matter was carried on so cunningly, that those who knew *Mustapha*, and saw him lie dead before his Father's Tent, yet were afraid to believe their own Eyes, but suffered themselves to be persuaded, that this was the true *Mustapha* indeed: Yea, some of *Mustapha*'s Intimates, who knew this was but a Cheat, were yet so overfond of his Memory, that, blinded either with Fear, Grief, or Anger, they were the first that listed themselves under this *Pseudo-Mustapha*, as being weary of their Lives without him; which made others certainly think, that this was the true *Mustapha* indeed, whom Report had falsely given out to be slain. And, besides, the Impostor himself, by large Promises and great Presents, which he said were the Relicks of his former Acquisitions, (but indeed were the Supplies that *Bajazet* had provided under-hand) did not cease to cajole and engage his Followers. So that in a very few Days he got a handsome body of Men together, fit for a little Army; and they encreased every day.

WHEN *Solyman* was made acquainted by Messages and Letters, which the neighbouring *Sanziacks*, had, in great trepidation, sent him, what hazard he was in by reason of the resort of such Multitudes, to this *Pseudo-Mustapha*; the cunning old Man knew one of his Sons must needs be privy to the Plot, and therefore, he made haste to disappoint it; chiding his *Sanziacks*, by Letter, that they suffered the Matter to come to such a Head, and had not rather crush'd the Cockatrice in the Egg; but, seeing they had been negligent hitherto, he commanded them to make amends for their former Remissness, and to send him presently, the Traitor and his Followers, Prisoners, in Chains, to receive their condign Punishment; and, to facilitate the Matter, he would send Aid to them, by one of his *Viziers, Partan Bassa* who had married the Widow of *Mahomet* aforesaid. However, he advised them, if they would purge themselves of their criminal Neglect, they should quell the Insurrection before his Succour came. *Partan* had but a few Troops with him; but they were choice Men, eminent for Courage and

Faithfulness. *Solyman* took care to cull out Colonels, Captains, and other Commanders of that Inclination for this Service, as suspecting that others might have been corrupted, or enticed to pass over to the Tents of the Rebels; for, the Truth was, the ordinary sort of *Janizaries*, upon account of *Mustapha*'s Name, did not seem much averse from the Party; and, therefore, did not care what further Confusions might enhance the Danger on that side.

The *Sanziacks*, as soon as ever they received *Solyman*'s threatning Dispatches, began to bestir themselves, and to rouze up one another so that happy was he, that could do most Damage to the growing Party of the Impostor. Some of those that were going in to him, they intercepted; those that had already join'd him, they laboured to discourage by terrible Menaces and Denunciations of the Danger they were in. In the mean time, the Forces of *Partan Bassa* were marching on, and being almost come up to the Place, the Party of the Tumultuous, which were not yet fully settled, seeing so great Preparations, made against them, began to be discouraged, (as is usual with Men in such Circumstances) and to drop off one by one; and at last the whole Body of them most shamefully left their Leader, and shifted for themselves, the belt they could. Their feigned *Mustapha*, with his chief Partisans and Setters on, would willingly have done so too; but he was so watch'd by the *Janizaries*, that he was taken alive, and sent Prisoner to *Partan*, who, with a strong Guard, sent him to *Constantinople*. When he came thither, *Solyman* put him on the Rack, and by that means found out the whole Plot; how his Son *Bajazet* was at the bottom of it, and had resolved, if they had not been so soon dissipated, to have join'd them with a considerable Force, and so either to have marched directly to *Constantinople*, or else (if Opportunity had served him) to have fought out his Brother; but being slow in his Actings, his Design was nipp'd in the very Bud. When *Solyman* had thus ferreted out the Design to the bottom, he caused him and his Abettors to be thrown into the Sea at Midnight, not thinking it convenient to have the Matter divulg'd among his own People, or that foreign Princes should be acquainted with the domestic Differences of his own Family.

As for his Son *Bajazet*, he was mightily exasperated against him for his foul Offence, and was meditating in his Mind what grievous Punishment he should inflict upon him. In the mean time, his Wife being a prying Woman, and therefore allowing him but little space for his Anger to vent and cool itself, at last falling into Discourse with him of the Affair, she began to excuse her Son, laying all the Fault on his youthful Imprudence; and that some of his Ancestors also had been necessitated to undertake the like Attempts. For (says she) 'tis a natural Instinct in all Men to do what they can for themselves and their Friends, and to save their Lives, if they can; especially, young Men, in the fervour of Youth, are apt to be drawn aside by ill Counsellors to pernicious Attempts; and, therefore, it was but reasonable that his first Fault should be pardoned, because, if he repented, his Father had gained a great Point in preserving his Son; but if he relapsed again into the same Crime, then the Father was at liberty to inflict deserved Punishment on him, for both Offences, at one and the same time. But, proceeded she, if you will not pardon him for his own sake, yet be pleased to do it for mine; and spare our own common Flesh and Blood: For how, think you, can I bear it, that, of two Sons which God hath yet left me, your Severity should rend one of them from me? And, therefore, she intreated him to moderate his Anger, and not to let loose the Reins to Cruelty, though he had never so just an Occasion. Almighty God (said she) though most Powerful and Just, yet doth not always exert his highest Severities, but tempers them with Indulgence, else Mankind would be quickly destroyed. And, if Clemency may be shew'd to any, to whom, pray, more properly than to a Man's own Children? *Bajazet*, for the future, will certainly keep within the bounds of his Duty, and the Fear, wherein he now is, will certainly be turned into the highest Degree of filial Obedience for the future. If you please to spare his Life, the Sense of your Indulgence will work this; for nothing is so obliging to generous Minds as Courtesies received. The Memory of his Pardon will restrain him from running a second time into the like Offence; and I my self will undertake for him, that for the future he will carry it towards you, as a most dutiful and obedient Son.

To these Intreaties she added Tears and Caresses, so that the old Man, who was Uxorious enough before, could no longer withstand her Importunities, but changed his Mind; and, instead of punishing, resolved to pardon his Son; but on this Condition, that he was to come into his Presence, and receive his Commands. His Mother, being exceeding glad at the good Success of her Interposal, was not wanting to the Occasion; but presently acquainted *Bajazet* by Letters that, whenever he was sent for, he should not scruple in the least to come to his Father, for she had wrought a

Reconciliation betwixt them, so that not the least spark of Discontent lay now covered in his Mind against him. Upon the Receipt of this good News, *Bajazet* resolves to trust his Father, yet not without some Relicks of Fear; he reflected ever and anon on his Brother *Mustapha*, whose Example warned him of the Danger he underwent. However, conquering his Fear, come he did to the place of Conference appointed by his Father; it was called *Carestrane*, some few Miles distant from *Constantinople*.

You must know; that, now-a-days, 'tis the custom of the *Turkish* Emperors, never to permit any one of their Sons, when once they are grown up, to set their Foot within the Gates of *Constantinople*, (whilst they are alive) for fear they should ingratiate themselves with the Soldiery, and so set up for themselves. As he was alighting from his Horse, some of his Father's Servants were at hand to take away his Sword and Dagger. This struck his guilty Conscience into a little Fear, though it were accustomed to be done to others, that they might come unarmed into their Emperor's Presence: But his Mother, who had placed her self on purpose near his Passage, looked out at a Window, using these Expressions, *Chear up, chear up, my Son!* By which Antidote he was very much heartened and relieved.

As soon as ever he came into his Father's Presence, the old Man bid him sit down, and then began to blame him very severely for his Rashness, in taking up Arms so causelesly. They may be looked upon, said he, as taken up against my self: But, grant you took them up only against your Brother, yet it takes off little from your Offence; for, if you had had your Wish, the *Ottoman* Religion would have been quite shaken, if not overthrown, by the domestic Discords among our Family, (on the Heirs whereof it doth depend); so that, if you be a true *Mussulman*, such a Crime ought to have been far from your Thoughts. I might aggravate your Crime (said he) by telling you, that you aspired to the Government in my Life-time, which is so contemptuous a Thing, that your Offence is almost inexpiable: Nevertheless, I am resolved to pardon you, and to shew my self a loving Father, rather than a just Judge, that so for the future you may leave all to God; for Kingdoms, and the Governments of them are not disposed of by Man's Pleasure, but by the Will of God. If he hath decreed that you shall have the Kingdom after me, no Man living will be able to hinder it: But, if God had otherwise determined, 'twas a mad Thing in you to go about to resist his Will; for that were to fight against God. And, therefore, let me advise you to be quiet; and not disturb your peaceable Brother, nor interrupt the Quiet of my old Age; for, I will assure you, if you commit a second Offence of this Nature, I will be so far from Pardoning you, that you shall have the Severity of Justice.

BAJAZET's Answer was very submissive, acknowledging his Fault, and promising Subjection for the future. Whereupon *Solyman* called for Drink, and caused it to be given to his Son, (as the Custom is) which was a Sherbet, made of Sugar, and the Juice of certain Fruit. *Bajazet* had rather have let it alone, as fearing it might have been his last Draught, but he could not handsomely refuse it: So he drank a little, and his Father drank a little after him; which freed him of his Fear. Thus *Bajazet* was dismissed, and sent away to his Government, his Congress with his Father having been far more auspicious, than his Brother *Mustapha*'s was.

As for the Death of *Achmet Bassa*, another of your Enquiries, I shall give this short Relation. Some say, he was put to Death for being too much affected to *Mustapha*, and for favouring underhand the counterfeit *Mustapha*, and encouraging *Bajazet* in his Designs. Others say, that being a mere Robber or Swash-Buckler at first, but advanced for his Audacity, Valour and Skill in military Affairs, to that high Dignity, the Punishment of his former flagitious Life, was only deferred to the last Period of it. And some were of Opinion, he was executed only to make Way for *Rustan*; for *Solyman*, having promised *Achmet* never to take away the Seal from him, so long as he lived, to make a collusive Performance of his Word, he caused him to be put to Death, before he did it. Some said, that *Solyman* gave it out, 'Twas better to die once, than a thousand Times over; for the Fear of the Loss of his *Grand Viziership*, and much more his Survival thereupon, would have been as a thousand Deaths to him. Whatever was the Cause, the Manner of it was this: He came early in the Morning into the Divan, (or Council-Chamber) being ignorant of what was designed against him: By and by comes the Messenger to him from the *Sultan*, telling him, that he must die. He was a Man of a great Spirit, and received the Message as undauntedly, as if it had nothing concerned him; only, when the Executioner drew near, to do his Office, he pushed him away, as thinking it dishonourable for a Man of his Dignity to die by the Hands of an ordinary Executioner: But, casting his Eyes round about the Company, he espied a creditable Person, that was his Friend; him he desired to do that last Office for him, and he should take it as a great Kindness at his Hands. His Friend, upon his iterated Request, undertook it: Only *Achmet* advised, not to draw the Cord, or Bow-string, so as to dispatch him at once, but when he had strained it a little, then to remit it, that he might breath a while, and afterwards to pull it as hard as he could, until he were dead; wherein his Desire was answered. Thus *Achmet* was willing to taste (as it were) of Death, before he drank his full Draught of it. Upon his Decease *Rustan* had the *Grand-Viziership* bestowed upon him.

As for my Return out of this Country, which you desire to hear of, all I can say is, *Facilis descensus Averni.* He that brought me hither, will, when he sees good, bring me back: In the Interim, I solace my self in the Company of my old Friends, my Books, which never fail to afford me Relief both Day and Night.

Constantinople, June 12.

SIR,

WHAT you have heard, is very true, in every particular; for it is most certain, that all my Collegues are returned Home, and poor I am left behind, alone. And, whereas you put several Questions to me, as, what Fate, or what malevolent Star, kept me back from accompanying them in their Return? And why I did not shake Hands with that barbarous Country, to enjoy the wish'd for Comforts of my own? And withal, you demand, what memorable Matters I have seen or heard of since I wrote last? Promising to give Credit to whatever drops from my Pen, as if it were as true as Gospel. And moreover, you desire to know the course of my Studies, and how I relieve my self, both in my Solitudes and Sufferings? And whether I go abroad, or always stay at home? All these Demands put together, will engage me to write rather Commentaries or Diaries, than a single Letter, especially, since you are very earnest to know, how *Bajazet*'s Matters stand, concerning which, you say, there are various Reports with you. You claim a Promise from me, and unless I perform it, you tell me you will commence an Action against me, and have already drawn your Breviat. To pursue your Metaphor, let me persuade you to stay a while, *Leniter qui sæviunt, sapiunt magis*, says the old Proverb, no Haste to kill true Men: But if you are so much given to Law, take Use and Principal too, rather than I will answer your Suit, for I am averse from *Lawing*. And besides, the distance of Place is so great between us, that if I should put in an Exception to your *Plea*, yet your Writ would hardly abate. But, however it be, I will rather satisfy your Desires, than contend with you in the least. When my Collegues (whose Names I gave you in my last Letters) perceived, that our three Years Abode in this Place had produced little Good hitherto, either to the making of a firm Peace, or the continuing the Truce; and that small Hopes of either did appear for the future, they laboured with Might and Main to be dismissed by this Court; and when, with much ado, *Solyman*'s Consent was obtained therein, (for 'tis no easy matter to get a Dismission from hence) the only Question was, whether we should all go, or only those of us that came first, and so had been longest there? For cunning *Solyman*, that he might not seem over desirous of Peace, by retaining one of us, remitted the Matter wholly to our own Choice. In these Circumstances, my Companions thought it very adviseable, and for our Master's Service, that one of us should stay behind; and I my self was of the same Mind: But we resolved to dissemble our Sentiments, and conceal them from the *Turks*, so that, as often as we had any Discourse with them on that Subject, I always pretended an utter Unwillingness to stay behind. 'Tis true, I told them I came thither to reside as Ambassador in Ordinary; but it was on Supposition, that Peace would be made between both Empires. That not being yet done, I did not see how I could well stay, but to the Damage, and against the Will of my Master, and therefore it was best that we should all return together. Thus I reasoned before them, that so I might stay on better Terms, rather by their Entreaty than by my own voluntary Offer. I knew well enough, that, if we all went away, it would not only open a wide Door for a War, but it would even quite shut out all Hopes of Peace; which latter was not despaired of, if I staid behind: For, whilst Dispatches were sent to and from both Princes, it would spin out a great deal of Time, in which Interval something or other might fall out of advantage to our Cause; so that it was better to do any thing, than to precipitate our selves into a fierce and cruel War; and yet I was not ignorant, how prejudicial my Stay would be to my self, for thereby my Care and Labour would be doubled, in regard one was to do the Work of two or three: Besides, many Inconveniencies might occasionally arise, especially, if the Issue of my Transactions did terminate in a War: And yet, I must tell you, he that undertakes the Office of a public Ambassador, must post-pone all such private Difficulties, and make light of them, in comparison of the public Good of his Prince and Country. And I had a fair Opportunity to manage this Affair by the Complaisance of *Rustan*, who was very desirous of my Stay; for that subtle *Vizier* easily foresaw, what a shrewd Step towards a War it would be, if we should all be gone and leave the Negotiation for a Peace unfinished. The old Fox was averse from War, upon this Account principally; he foresaw that, if *Solyman* made an Expedition into *Hungary*, it was impossible to prevent the Discords of his Children; for if *Selimus* were willing to be quiet, yet *Bajazet* would attempt Innovation, especially since he was favoured by himself, his Wife, and Mother-in-law; and such Commotions, he knew, would be fatal to him: And therefore, when we were once at his House, he made a long Harangue to my Colleagues, advising them what to say to their Master at their Return, in order to a Peace. As for me, he advised me by all means to stay behind, and not to desert a Business so well begun, till it came to the desired Issue; and there's no doubt, said he, but the Emperor, your Master, who always shewed himself inclining to Peace, will approve well-enough of your Stay. However, I continued deaf to his Request, as far as with Safety I could, and insisted on my Return; which egg'd him on the more, to persuade me to stay: What, says he, will you cut off all Hopes of Peace for ever? Our Emperor longs for nothing more than to send an Army into *Hungary*, and he had long since done it, if I had not made use of some female Instruments (meaning his Wife and Mother-in-law) to dissuade him; yea, as it were to pluck him back by the Sleeve; and therefore, if you be wife, don't rouze a sleeping Lyon to destroy you. Upon this I began to yield a little, and was less peremptory in my Refusal to stay; only I told them, my greatest Remora was, I was afraid of their unjust Reproaches; that, if Matters succeeded not as they would have them, the whole Blame would be cast upon me (though it was not in my Power to help it) and therefore they would make me feel the Fruits of their Indignation. But *Rustan* bid me be of good Cheer, whatever the Event were; if unsuccessful, it should not be imputed to me; if I would but stay, he promised to take me under his Protection, and next he would treat me (to use his own Words) as if I were his natural Brother. I told him, I would consider of it; and so we parted for that Time.

THE next Day we were called into the *Divan*, (so they called their Council-Chamber) and then the same Part was acted over again; only *Rustan* carried it a little more covertly, and reservedly, because of the Presence of other *Bashaws*. There, at last, I yeilded to stay behind, only leaving a Memorial with them of this Import, that I staid behind unknown to my Master, and therefore I would leave all my Concessions to his Arbitrement, to cancel or confirm: As for myself, I would be responsible for nothing, nor oblige myself by any Promise, whatever issue God were pleased to give of my Negotiation. This Memorial was of great Service to me afterwards, in difficult Circumstances, so that the *Bashaws* could not, for shame, treat me so severely in their Resentments, as otherwise they would have done.

THUS, Sir, you have an Account of my Stay behind my Fellows, with the Reason of it. They left *Constantinople* about the latter end of *August*, 1557. The Winter following, the *Grand Seignior* went to *Adrianople*, as his Custom was, both to strike a greater Terror into *Hungary*, upon the Report of his nearer approach thither, and also for the Conveniencies of his Hunting, (for there the Winters are colder than at *Constantinople*,) both which he thought conducive to his Health. The Country thereabout is full of Marshes and Stagnant Waters, by reason of the nearness of many Rivers; so that there are abundance of Water-Fowl, as wild-Ducks, Geese, Herons, Storks, Cranes, Bitterns, &c. To catch them, he makes use of Hawks, or a lesser sort of Eagles, which are so used to the Sport, that, though the Fowl fly up to the Clouds, they'll fetch him down from thence; but, if they fly lower, then they truss them, and with a mighty Force strike them with their Bills to the Ground. I am told, that some of his Falcons are so disciplin'd and expert, that they will venture on a Crane, even in that part of the Body where the Wing joyns it; and by this means the Crane's Bill can do them no hurt, and so they tumble to the Ground with their Prey: And yet sometimes the Hawk pays dear for his Boldness; for, if he do but miss his Gripe never so little, presently the Crane runs him through with his Bill, and down he tumbles dead to the Ground.

For this Reason, the *Grand Seignior* ordinarily every Year, a little before Winter, goes to *Adrianople*, and returns not again to *Constantinople*, till the Frogs begin to be troublesome to him by their croaking. Thither *Rustan*, a while after, sent for me by Letter; he appointed some Horse to guard me on the Way, and Sixteen *Janizaries*; whether as a Guard to me, or upon me, I leave to you to judge. We made long Journeys; for he advised us to make hast. On the Third Day my *Janizaries*, being on Foot, began to grumble; the Ways were dirty, as is usual at that Time of the Year, and they complained, that they were often forced to march more Miles in a Day, than they were used to do; and that, if their Emperor were there, they could hardly endure it.

Their Complaints troubled me not a little, because I was loth to disoblige this sort of People, and therefore I consulted with my Servants, how I might allay their Discontents, and make them willinger to Travel. One of mine told me, he had observed that they were much taken with a certain kind of Caudle, Gruel or Pottage, which my Cook used to make of Wine, Eggs, Sugar and Spices: Perhaps (says he) if they have some of that for their Break-fast, they will be plyable. This seemed but a mean Expedient, yet we resolved to try it, and the Success answered our Expectation; for, after this sweet Soop, it being also further heated with a Glass or two of Wine, away they trudged as merrily as could be, and told me, they would accompany me, on the same Terms, to *Buda*, if I pleased.

WHEN I came to *Adrianople*, I was forced to hear the Railings, rather than the Complaints of *Rustan*, concerning the plundering Excursions of the *Hungarians*. And, by way of Answer, I was as ready to complain to him of the frequent Depredations and Mischiefs, which the *Turks* did in *Christian* Countries. No marvel, said I, if we retort like for like; for I had just then received an Express from *Cæsar*, my Master, informing me, what Breaches and Contraventions the *Turks* had made of that Truce, which at the Departure of my Collegues, was agreed upon: How they vexed the poor Peasants with continual Inrodes, robbing them of their Goods, and made themselves, their Wives and Children, Slaves.

I must not forget to acquaint you, that the same Day, a Messenger came to me with an Express from *Cæsar*, my Master. There happened an Earthquake at *Adrianople*, from which he took an occasion to tell me, that he perceived the same (so he judged it) at *Nissa, S. Sophia* and other Places through which he Travelled, so that the Air, included in the Bowels of the Earth, did seem to have kept Pace with him, by some subterraneous Passages or Caverns, and to have travelled as far in a Day under Ground, as he himself had done on the Surface of it. This Conjecture afterward seemed to be confirmed, upon the Relation we received of an Earthquake that happened in *Constantinople* four Days after, which seemed to be the same imprisoned Air, that had made its Way, under Ground, even to that City also.

I leave the Matter to your Judgment; but this is certain, that Earthquakes are very frequent at *Constantinople*; for once, when I was there, about Mid-Night, my Lodgings did so shake, that it was almost ready to fall. This Accident awakened me, though fast asleep, and, having a Watch-Light burning by me all Night, when I saw here a Cup, there a Book, a Table, Board and Stone all tumbled in a Heap together, I was at first astonished at the Novelty of the Spectacle, till I had recollected myself; and judging it to be the Effects of an Earthquake, I then retired to that part of the House which I thought most secure from falling. The same Commotion of the Earth continued some Days, but not with like Violence. Yea, over all that great City, and especially in my Lodgings, and in the Temple of S. *Sophia*, you might see the Walls, though very thick, to crack and gape by reason of the Clefts made by such Earthquakes.

WELL; I staid about three Months at *Adrianople*, made a Truce there for Seven Months, and in *March* was attended back again to *Constantinople*. When I came thither, I was quite weary of being mew'd up in my old Lodging, it was so close, and therefore I dealt with my *Chiaux*, (a sort of Officers among the *Turks*, which serve for divers Employments, of which Attendance on Ambassadors is one) that I might have Liberty, as other Ambassadors had before me, to hire an House at my own Charge, where I may have the Benefits of Gardens, Orchards, and a free Air to breath in. The *Chiaux* was not averse to my Proposal, for he saw that the *Grand Seignior*'s Interest was concerned therein, who was wont to hire Houses for Ambassadors, at the yearly Rent of 400 Ducats; and now all that Expence would be saved: Hereupon I went to a House, or Island rather, hired with my own Money, where there was a broad Field adjoyning, which I resolved to turn into a Garden, and to relieve my wearisom Embassy, in managing and planting it: But, see the Spight of it! When the *Chiaux* found, by Experience, that he could not have so strict an Eye over me in an open House that had many Ways to it, with a large space of Ground near it, as he had in a *Caravansera* (which Word you know the meaning of, by my former Letters) because this latter was fenced with Cross-barr'd Windows, and, besides, had but one Passage into it, he began to change his Mind, and thereupon made his Address to the *Bashaws*, who by this Time were returned from *Adrianople*, that I might retire from my former Lodging: And I was to look upon this as a great Courtesy too; for some of the *Bashaws*, in a Debate betwixt them, concerning the Disposal of me, were of Opinion, that, now I was alone, a less House would serve my turn, and so some Charge might be saved; But the more moderate Party carried it, that I should return to my old Quarters.

IF you desire a Description of the House I lodged in, take it thus. It is situate on a Rising Ground, in the most celebrated part of *Constantinople*; in the Back-side of it there is a pleasant, but somewhat distant, Prospect to the Sea, which yet is not so remote from it, but that you may easily discern the Dolphins skipping and playing therein: And also at a vast distance a Man may see Mount *Olympus* in *Asia*, which wears a snowy-white Cap all the Year; it lies open to the Wind from every Quarter, which by ventilating the Air, makes it more wholsom and healthy. But the *Turks* are so envious to their *Christian* Tenants, that they would cut them off from as many Conveniencies as they can, and therefore they do not only set Iron Grates before their Windows, but also add Iron Boards and Planks to hinder the Prospect, and the free Passage of their Air; and by this means they stop the Mouths of Neighbouring *Turks*, who are apt to complain, that they can do nothing in their Houses but the Christians must overlook them. The House is built in a Quadrangular Form, with a large Square in the midst, wherein there is a Well.

THE upper part of the House, which is all of it that is inhabited, is divided into Galleries, which go round it, and into Lodging Chambers. The Galleries look down into the Quadrangle within, and without are the Lodgings, which have all a Passage into them; there are a great many of them, but they are small and uniform, as the Cells or Chambers of Monks are with us. The Front stands over against the High Way leading to the *Seraglio*; and the *Grand Seignior*, every *Friday* (which is their Sabbath, as the Lord's Day is with us) passes by it to his Devotions, so that Ambassadors may easily see him out of their Windows. And the Family, together with the *Chiaux* and the *Janizaries*, do obeysance to him in the Porch, or do re-salute him rather; for the Fashion of the *Turks* is, that the Greater doth first of all salute the Less, and therefore the *Grand Seignior* as he passes, first salutes the People with a Nod of his Head; and then they very officiously pay their Court to him, with Acclamations and Shouts.

THE lower Part of the House is designed for the Stabling of Horses; and, to preserve it from Fire within, it is all built with Vaults or arched Roofs, and without it is covered with Lead. 'Tis true, such kind of Building hath some Advantages; and it hath as many Inconveniencies to ballance them: For all things are made therein for necessary Use, but nothing for Delight and Pleasure. There is nothing of Beauty or Novelty that can entertain your Fancy; no Garden belonging to it, to give a Man the Pleasure of a Walk; there is neither Tree, Shrub nor green Herb, to delight your Eye; you have only many wild Beasts as your troublesome Inmates and Companions. Snakes you have in abundance, store of Weesels, Lizards and Scorpions; so that sometimes when you would fetch your Hat in the Morning, from the Place you left it in the Night before, you find it surrounded with a Snake, as with a terrible Hat-Band; And yet these Animals afforded me some kind of Diversion in my Solitude, (for you must give me leave to tell you all my Entertainments). I once saw a Weesel fiercely combating with a Snake, and though the whole Family look'd upon her, yet she was not terrified therewith; but though her Adversary struggled, and made what Defence he could, yet she victoriously haled him into her Hole. Another Time I saw a Weesel carrying her young Weesling from one part of the House to another; and, as she was so doing, she leap'd down upon the middle of the Table, where I and some of my Guests were sitting after Dinner, having the young one in her Mouth, which she very fairly left among us on the Table, and skip'd no farther than the Door, as if she had waited what Event would betide her Youngling. When we had satisfied ourselves with the Sight of that (yet sharpless) Animal, we laid it down upon the Ground, and then the Dam ran hastily, and snatching it up, carried it to her desired Place. Another time I saw either a Snake, or a Dragon, or a Serpent, trod to pieces by the Horse's Feet, in the Stable; her Belly was very big, and, after I had caused it to be opened, I found three huge Mice therein. 'Twas a wonder to me, how such a slow and creeping Animal could catch so swift and so running a one; and, after he had catch'd him, how he could swallow him down, by reason of the narrowness of his Throat and Jaws. But my Wonderment was soon abated, when I beheld another Snake seize upon a mighty Toad; and, after he had him in his Mouth, he began at the hinder Part, and had devoured a great deal of it; and yet the Toad was still alive, and did what he could with his Fore-Feet to deliver himself from his Enemy. 'Twas in this very Posture, when I saw it first; which made me admire, and to be almost of the Opinion, that I saw a Monster, an Animal with two Feet, and a Tail as long as a Serpent; but when I drew nearer, and perceived what it was, I hit the Snake with my Staff, to make him let go his Prey, which at last he endeavoured to do, that he might creep the nimbler away; but, whether he would or no, the Toad stuck in his Throat; yet, at last, when with much-a-do, he had shaken him out, he could not shut his Mouth, but continued gaping, in an ugly Posture, till we killed him. Such a Staff, if we may believe *Pliny*, hath a kind of magical Virtue to help Child-bearing Women in the Time of their Labour.

But, for my Part, I was not content with the Native Animals of that Country, but fill'd my House with Outlandish ones too; and my Family busied themselves, by my Order, to our mutual Contents, in feeding them, that we might the better bear the Absence from our own Country: For seeing we were debarred of human Society, what better Conversation could we have to drive Grief out of our Minds, than among wild Beasts?

Otherwise, Stones, Walls and Solitudes had been but lamentable Amusements for us.

AMONGST these, Apes led the Van, which making us good Sport, occasioned great Laughter amongst us, and therefore you should seldom see them without a whole Ring of my People about them, delighting to observe their antick Tricks and Gestures. I also bred up some Wolves, some Bears, some broad-horned Stags (vulgarly miscalled, Bucks) and common Deers; also Hinds, Lynx's, Ichneumons or *Indian* Rats, Weesels of that sort which you call Ferrets and Fairies: And, if you would know all, I kept also a Hog, whose noisome Smell was wholsome for my Horses, as my Grooms persuaded me: So that, in my Nomenclature of other Creatures, 'tis not fit I should omit my Hog, which made my House to be mightily frequented by the *Asiaticks*. They came thick and three-fold to see that Creature, which is counted unclean by them, and by the Books of their Religion they are forbid to eat it, so that, it being a prohibited Animal among them, they never saw one before. Yea, all *Turks* are as much afraid to touch a Hog, as Christians are to come near to those who are infected with the Plague. This Humour of theirs being known, we put a pretty Trick upon them; when any body had a mind to send me a secret Message, which he would not have my *Chiaux* know of, he put it into a little Bag, together with a Roasting-Pig, and send it by a Youth: When my *Chiaux* met him, he would ask, what he had there? Then the Boy, being instructed before, whisper'd him in the Ear, and say, that a Friend of mine had sent me a Roasting-Pig, for a Present: The *Chiaux*, thereupon, would punch the Bag with his Stick, to see whether the Boy spake Truth or no; and when he heard the Pig grunt, he would run back as far as ever he could, saying, *Get thee in, with the nasty Present!* Then, spitting on the Ground, and turning to his Fellows, he would say; *'Tis strange to see how these Christians do dote on this filthy impure Beast; they cannot forbear eating of it, though their Lives lay at stake.* Thus he was handsomely choused, and the Boy brought me what secret Message was sent me. I kept also a great many sorts of Birds, as Eagles, Jack-daws, *Muscovy* Ducks, *Balearick* Cranes, and Partridges; yea, my House is so full of them, that, if a Painter were to draw it, he may take from thence the Copy of *Noah*'s Ark. Besides the Delight that I and my Family take in these Creatures, to counterpoise our long Absence from our own Country, I got also this Advantage by them, that now I know, by Experience, what I could hardly believe when I read it in Books. You know a great many Books are full of strange Stories, what ardent Love some wild Beasts have to Mankind: I could never give Credit to such Relations, but looked upon them as Romances, till I saw with my Eyes, a Lynx, which I got out of *Assyria*, so passionately affected towards one of my Servants, though known to him but a little while before, that for my part I could not think but she was in Love with him: For, whenever he was present, she would mightily fawn upon him, and in a manner embrace him, and almost kiss him. Whenever she was about to go away from him, she would gently lay her Claws on his Cloaths, as labouring to retain him; and, when he was gone, she would eye him; and whensoever he was in Sight, would hardly ever remove her Eye from that Quarter. During the Time of his Absence, she was very sad, but upon his Return she would skip and be jocund; she could not endure he should be at any Time absent; for one Time, when he went with me beyond Sea, to the *Turkish* Camp, the Lynx pined away by degrees, would not eat a bit, but at length died.

I was troubled for his Loss, for I had designed him, with another choice Ichneumon (which I had) as a Present for my Master *Cæsar*; and the rather, because of the exceeding Beauty of his Skin, which made him look quite different from other Lynxes: The best of the kind are bred in *Assyria*, from whence this came, and their Skins are sold here for fifteen or sixteen Crowns of Gold apiece. I question not, but these were the *Babilonian* Pells or Skins, so much famed and valued amongst the Ancients, of which mention is made in Law-Books; in the Title of *Publicans*.

IF you please to hear me, I'll tell you another story of a Bird: I have, among my other Birds, a *Balearic* Crane, which differs from the ordinary sort of Cranes by a white Plume of Feathers, that grows hanging down from both her Ears; and besides, all the fore-part of her Neck-Feathers were black, and the *Turks* adorn their Turbants with it; and there is some Difference in their Bigness. This *Balearic* Bird was mightily affected with a *Spanish* Soldier, whom I had redeemed out of his Chains; when he walked abroad, the Bird would walk with him, though for many Hours together; when he stood still, so did the Crane; when he sat down, she would stand by him, and suffer him to handle her, and stroke down her Feathers, whereas she would not suffer any body else so much as to touch her; whenever he was gone from Home, she would come to his Chamber-door and knock against it with her Beak; if any body open'd it, she would look all about, to see whether he were in the Room; and, not finding him, she would traverse it about, making such a shrill Din and Noise, that nothing living could endure it; so that we were forced to shut her up, that her Noise might not offend us. But when he returned, as soon as ever she fixed her Eyes on him, she would make to him, clapping her Wings with such an antick Posture of her Body as Dancers in a Jig use to do; or as if she had been to prepare herself for Combat with a Pygmy. In fine, she at last used to lie under his Bed at Night, where she laid him an Egg. Thus I have given the story of the Loves of brute Animals towards Man, now prepare your Ears for another Story of a contrary Import, *viz.* the Cruelty and Ingratitude of another Brute towards Man. I had a Hart, that lived very quiet and tame with me for many Months; but, when her rutting or coupling Time came, she grew on a sudden so wild, that, forgetting all our Respects, she flew upon every body that she met, as if she would have killed them with her Horns, so that we were compelled, for our own Security, to hamper her, and to shut her up in a walled Place; but one Night, she broke from her Prison, and ran amongst all the Horses, which, as I told you, in *Turkey*, use to stand all Night in the Yard, and where she made such a Tumult amongst them, that she forced the Grooms to drive her to her Hold; she wounded many of them, which set them into a Rage, so that at last they drove her into a large Stable, and there I gave them leave, with what Weapons came next to hand, to destroy her: She defended her self stoutly at first; but they, being forty to one, at last felled her, and made her pay for her breach of Hospitality. When she was dead, I cut her in pieces, and made a Feast for the Ambassadors that then resided at *Constantinople*. It was a Hart or Stag, of a huge Bulk, such as use to come in the beginning of *Autumn*, out of *Hungary* into *Austria*, at rutting Times. I bought him of some Beggars, that made a Gain of that Trade; they used to carry him about, and where they ask'd Alms for God's Sake, at the name of God they used to bow their Heads, and the Stag by Custom had learned to do so too; so that the Vulgar did admire the Beast, as if he had some Sense of a Deity, and therefore he got a deal of Gain to his Keepers. This Stag, by reason of his Talness, I also designed as a Present to *Cæsar*.

HAVING made mention of *Turkish* Beggars, give me leave to acquaint you with the nature of those kind of People in this Country. There are fewer Beggars here than amongst us, and they are commonly Pilgrims that travel up and down, pretending some appearance of Piety or religious Profession. Some of them, besides their Poverty, pretend Distraction and Simplicity;

and this sort is very much esteemed among them, for the *Turks* count all Madmen and Fools to be certainly designed for Heaven; and therefore they look upon them as Demi-Gods here on Earth. Some of those Wanderers are *Arabians*, who carry Banners before them, wherewith, as they say, their Ancestors fought against the Christians, for the Propagation of the *Mussulman* Religion. Those that are of this Rank are not ordinary Beggars, neither do they ask Alms of all Passengers, but in the Evening they offer you a Tallow-Candle, a Lemon or a Pomegranate, and force it upon you; but you must give them double or treble the Worth; and by this means they seem rather to sell than to receive *gratis*. For the rest, they which beg amongst Christians are set to do servile Offices amongst the *Turks*. If a Slave become lame, his Master is bound to maintain him, and yet the veriest Cripple amongst them brings in his Master some Profit. I remember, once I redeemed a *Spanish* Officer, bought by a *Turk*, who was maimed in all his Limbs, by reason of his Wounds, and yet his Master found means how to make him get his Living; he sent him over into *Asia*, to look to the Flocks of Geese which he kept there; and by his Care in feeding them, he brought in sufficient Gain to his Matter.

Now we talk of Slaves, give me leave to digress a little, and to propose a *Quære*, whether he did well or ill with *Christendom*, who first brought up the use of Slaves among them? I know there are many Inconveniencies that attend the Condition of Slaves, but they are over-balanced by the Advantages accruing thereby; especially if a just and merciful Slavery were allowed by some public Law, as was of old among the *Romans*; for then, perhaps, we should not need so many Gallows's and Gibbets as we have among us, to restrain those, who set an high Price on their Life and Liberty; to maintain which, their Poverty prompts them to the most audacious Attempts: Liberty, without an Estate to maintain it, is none of the best Counsellors. All Men cannot bear Poverty and Freedom; Mankind, in general, is not so form'd by Nature, as to rightly to govern himself. No, he stands in need of a better and wiser Conduct than his own; otherwise, there will be no end of his Transgressing; for so some Beasts will always be terrible to Men, unless their Fierceness be restrain'd by Manacles and Bonds. But in this case of Slavery, the weaker Mind of the Slave is govern'd and steer'd by the Authority of his Patron or Master; and, on the other side, the Master is maintained by the Labour of his Slave. The Truth is, both publickly and privately, the *Turks* make a very great Advantage of their Slaves; if any Houshold-work be to be done, the Slave is ready to perform it; and, therefore, they have a Proverb among them, *He can never be poor, that hath but one Slave*. But then for Works without Doors, if there be any Rubbish to be carried out, or Preparation made for any great Building, the assiduity of Slaves quickly performs what is enjoined them. This I take to be one Reason, why our present Buildings do not arrive to the Magnificence of the Ancients; we want Hands (or Slaves) to carry on the Work. I might instance also, that servile Hands and Heads have been great helps to the Learned, to attain their so much celebrated Learning and Knowledge. What I have hitherto discoursed about Slaves, you will look upon as an Amusement; and so, pray, take it.

THIS I can a assure you of, that the *Turks*, in their way, do make a huge Advantage of Slaves; for if an ordinary *Turk* bring home one or two Slaves, whom he hath taken Prisoners in War, he accounts he hath made a good Campaign of it, and his Prize is worth his Labour. An ordinary Slave is sold among them for 40 or 50 Crowns; but if he be young, beautiful, and have Skill in some Trade besides, then they rate him at twice as much. By this you may know, how advantageous the *Turkish* Depredations are to them, when many times, from one Expedition, they bring home five or six thousand Prisoners.

THE *Romans* of old, were not ignorant of this gainful Trade; which made them set an high Rate on 20 or 30 thousand Persons, which they sometimes took at the sacking of Cities, as their Writings shew. But a *Turk*, upon the like Sack, would make ten times five hundred Crowns of his Prize, though by the rules of their Religion they are not to make Slaves of any of their own Sect; nor to disfranchize them, or set any Price on their Heads.

BUT to return from this large Digression: I formerly acquainted you with my Sport in *Hunting*; it follows, in course, that I must say something of my *Fowling*. The *Turks* are favourable to all Beasts, as also to Birds; and especially to Kites, because, they say, they eat up the Carrion, and keep the Streets clean and wholsome; and, therefore, abundance of these Birds fly up and down the Town, as fearless of Gin or Snare, so that they are almost tame; and when you whistle to them, they come about you; throw them up Meat in the Air, they'll catch it with their Claws. Once I caused a Sheep to be killed, and called the Kites to prey upon the Entrails. I cut them in pieces, and threw them up into the Air; by and by came ten or twelve or twenty Kites, and a while after so many of them, that they almost shaded the House; and they are so bold, withal, that if you hold out a piece of Flesh, they will be ready to snatch it out of your Hands. In the mean time, I stood with my Cross-Bow behind the Pillar, and sometimes when I shot, I made the Tail or Feathers of one or other of them to fly off, and sometimes I gave one or two a mortal Wound, and made them tumble down; but this I did privately, when the Doors were shut, that so I might not provoke the *Turks* to Indignation.

I must tell you, I have *Partridges* too (to acquaint you with my whole Stock of pleasurable Recreations). You would wonder, as I my self did at first, how tame they are. They were brought from *Chios* with red Feet and Beaks; they were so troublesome to me, by standing at my Feet, and picking the Dust out of my Velvet Pantofle, with their Beaks, that they might dust themselves therewith, that, to be rid of the Molestation, I was forced to shut them up in a Chamber, where, in a short time, they grew over-fat and died, as my Servants told me; yet *Pliny* says, in a certain Place, that *Hares* and *Partridges* never grow fat. You have yet but small ground for your Wonderment; but, pray, prepare your Ears for what follows.

THE Isle of *Chios* is full of these Birds, and they live with the Inhabitants in their Houses; every Country-man, almost, keeps more or less of them under his Roof, as their Estates are, or their Minds serve them. A public Keeper whistles them out in a Morning, and they run to him in the Highway, and follow him into the Field (as Flocks of Sheep do their Shepherds with us): There they stay all Day to feed and bask themselves, and in the Evening he whistles for them again, and then they covey together, and return to their old Lodgings. The Custom arose from hence, as they say: As soon as ever the Partridges are hatch'd, the Country-men take them up and put them in their Bosoms, between their Skin and their Shirts; thus they carry them about a day or two, ever and anon moist'ning their Mouths with their own Spittle. This Courtesy doth so oblige the young Birds (for Partridges, as well as other Birds, are mindful of human Civilities, if I may so speak) that they cannot forget their Fosterers; and yet Care is to be taken, that they stay not out in the Field all Night; if they do so two or three times, they quickly forget human Hospitality, and return to their own natural free Life in the open Field. I have taken a great deal of Pains to procure such a Fosterer of Partridges to send him to *Cæsar*, to teach Emperors that aviary Discipline. 'Tis true, I never saw this done with my own Eyes; yet so many credible Witnesses have affirm'd the Truth thereof, and I believe it as well as if I had seen it. And I give equal Credit to the Story, I am now about to tell you.

It is so known a Truth in this Country, that he were an absurd Man that would offer to deny it. They that come to *Constantinople* from *Egypt*, (as many do continually) affirm it for certain, that Chicken are not hatched, as with us, by a Hen sitting abroad upon them, but there are some appointed Officers, that, in Spring-time, gather all the Eggs of the Neighbourhood and put them in a certain kind of Oven, which they make of Dung and Trash heaped up together, and by the heat of the Sun and the hot putrid Vapours, the Chicken in due time, are animated and break their Shells; and then the Owners come to claim the Chickens, which the Overseers of the Work deliver out to them, not by Tale, for that would be too tedious, but by Admeasurement. I mention this the rather, because I read of such a Passage in *Vopiscus*, where the Emperor *Adrian*, being angry with the *Egyptians*, inveighs against them with this Sarcasm; *I wish them*, says he, *no greater Curse, than that they may always feed on their own Chicken, which, how they are hatch'd, I am asham'd to tell.* So that, without Question, this was an old Custom among the *Egyptians*; and, therefore, *Adrian* upbraided them with their Food, which he looked upon as obscene, being begotten by Dung and Dirt. You may think, perhaps, that I am mistaken; but I leave the Matter with you, and shall now hasten to acquaint you with the rest of my Diversions.

Be pleased then to know, that I have also a breed of brave Horses; some from *Syria*, others from *Cilicia, Arabia, Cappadocia*, together with divers Camels, Sumpture-horses, and all Utensils fit for a Journey. For I would have the *Turks* believe, that I have now executed all my Master's Commands, and wait only for my Dismission to return home, which I press with great Importunity, knowing that, by reason of the present Discord among them, and the War between the two Brothers, I may obtain the better Conditions of Peace from them.

As I take Pleasure in my Horses on other Accounts, so especially when in an Evening I behold them brought, one by one, out of their Stables, and placed in the Yard, that so they may enjoy the Night-Air in Summer-time, and rest more sweetly. They march out so stately, shaking their Manes on their high Necks, as if they were proud to be seen; and they have Fetters on their Forefeet, and one of their hinder Feet is tied with a Cord to a Stake.

There is no Creature so gentle as a *Turkish* Horse; nor more respectful to his Master, or the Groom that dresses him. The reason is, because they treat their Horses with great Lenity. I my self saw when I was in *Pontus*, passing through a part of *Bithynia*, called *Axilos*, towards *Cappadocia*, how indulgent the Country-men were to young Colts, and how kindly they used them soon after they were foled; they would stroke them, bring them into their Parlours, and almost to their Tables, and use them even like Children. They hung something about their Necks, like a Jewel, even a Garter which was full of Amulets against Poison, which they are most afraid of; and the Grooms, that are to dress them, are as indulgent as their Masters; they frequently sleek them down with their Hands, and never use any Cudgel to bang their Sides, but in case of great Necessity. This makes their Horses great Lovers of Mankind; and they are so far from kicking, wincing, or growing untractable by this gentle usage, that you shall hardly find a masterless Horse among them.

But, alas! our Christian Grooms treat Horses at quite another rate; they never think them rightly curried, till they thunder at them with their Voice, and let their Club or Horse-whip, dwell, as it were, on their Sides. This makes some Horses even to tremble when their Keepers come into the Stable, so that they hate and fear them too: But the *Turks* love to have their Horses very gentle, that, at a word of Command, they may fall down on their Knees, and in this Posture receive their Riders.

They will take up a Staff or Club upon the Road, which their Rider hath let fall, with their Teeth, and hold it up to him again; and when they are perfect in this Lesson, then, for their Credit, they have Rings of Silver hung on their Nostrils, as a Badge of Honour and good Discipline. I saw some Horses, when their Master was fallen from the Saddle, that would stand Stock-still, without wagging a Foot, till he got up again. Another time, I saw a Groom standing at a distance, in the midst of a whole Ring of Horses about him, and, at a word of Command, they would either go round, or stand still. Once I saw some Horses, when their Master was at Dinner with me in an upper Room, prick up their Ears to hear his Voice; and when they did so, they neighed for Joy.

AND yet this is usual and common to all *Turkish* Horses, that they run forward with a stiff and stretch'd-out Neck, so that they cannot easily be stopp'd or hinder'd in their Course, but by fetching a large compass about. This in my Judgment, is the fault of the Bridles they wear, which all over *Turky* are of one Make, and not contrived harsher or tenderer, according to the Tenderness of the Horse's Mouth. I must also acquaint you, that the *Turks* do not Shoe their Horses as we *Christians* do; our Shoes are very open in the middle, but theirs are broad-web'd Shoes, that so their Feet may be less endangered in Travelling. Their Horses do also live longer than Ours.

I have seen a Horse of theirs as lusty at 20 Years old, as ours are at eight; yea, they say, in the Stables of the Emperor, there are Horses of 50 Years old; and which, for some great Merit, are exempt from Labour, and feed daily at the *Grand Seignior*'s Charge. The *Turks*, in Summer-nights, when the Weather is very hot, do not keep their Horses in their Stables, as we do; but cover their Backs with Horse-cloths, and so bring them forth into the open Air (as I told you before); and for Litter, they have only dry'd Horse-dung, which they save all the Year long, and spread under them for their Bedding: As for Straw, they make no use of it at all, either for Litter or Feed. Their usual Food is a little Hay, and a small quantity of Barley; with this Meat they grow not fat, for their Masters love lean Horses as being fitter for Race, and Burden, than foul-bodies ones. The cover them with Horse-cloths, both in the Winter and Summer, only they are thinner in One than in the Other. This contributes much to the smoothness of their Hair, and is also a good relief to their chilly Horses, which cannot endure the Cold.

IN those Steeds, as I lately told you, I take a great deal of Delight; when, about Sun-set, they are brought out of their Stables, and placed in a row in the Yard; where I call each Horse by his usual Name, as *Arabs*, *Caramanian*, &c. whereupon they fall a Neighing and give a Glance of their Eyes and stare at me. Sometimes I go down among them, and give to each of them a piece of Melon-rind out of my Hand, which makes them know me so well. Thus you see, what Shifts I am put to, to drive away my Melancholly.

I have also six She-Camels, which I keep by me, ready to carry my Baggage, as I pretend to the *Turks*; but my true Design is, to bring them to my Master the Emperor; if peradventure he, or other Christian Princes, may have a Fancy to breed out of them because of their great use.

There are two things which the *Turks* make mighty Advantage of, and those are *Rice* among the Fruits of the Earth, and *Camels* among the Beasts of the Field; both of them very convenient in their several Kinds, for long Expeditions. As for *Rice*, it is not easily spoil'd; it affords very wholsome Nourishment, and a little of it will serve a great many People. And for *Camels*, they'll carry huge Burdens; they will endure Hunger and Thirst to admiration; and also they require little Attendance. One Keeper will look after six or eight of them, and no Creature in the World is more obsequious to his Owner than the *Camel*; and for currying of them, they do it not with a Curry-Comb as we do, but with Brushes, as we do our wearing Apparel; they rather kneel than lie down, on the naked Ground; and in this Posture they offer themselves to be loaded; if you lay too much on their Backs they'll grumble a little, and refuse to rise; for their Backs will be easily broken under over-great Burdens, especially in Ways that are slippery and dirty. I was mightily pleased to see them stand all round in a Ring, and with their joined Heads, take Water or other Food, out of the same Bason or other Vessel, with such agreement among them. When Fodder is scarce, they live upon tops of Brambles or Thorns; and, when their Chops are bloodied in gathering them, they eat them down most sweetly.

The *Scythians* send a great many *Camels* to *Constantinople*; but the most part come from *China* and *Assyria*: From those Countries, there are whole Droves of them; and they are so cheap, that a *Mare* of a good Breed is worth an 100 *Camels*; wherein, perhaps, they respect more the Scarcity of *Mares* than the Cheapness of *Camels*; for good *Mares* are so scarce in that Country, that he that gets but one, of that sort, thinks himself a very *Crœsus* for Wealth. They try whether they are good or no, if they can run down a steep Hill, and not trip or stumble. When the *Grand Seignior* goes upon a Military Expedition into the Field, he carries above 40,000 of these *Camels* with him, and as many *Mules* for Burden; and these he loads with all sorts of Victuals, especially with *Rice*. They also carry Tents, Arms, and other Utensils of War, upon them; especially when he marches into *Persia*.

For, you must know, that the Countries over which the *Sophi*, or, as the *Turks* call him, *Chisilbas* of *Persia* reigns, are not so fruitful of Provisions, as our *European* Countries are. The Reason is, because the Custom of the

Inhabitants is, upon the Approach of an Enemy, to destroy all before them, that so Fire and Famine may send him farther off; so that if the Invader bring not great Store of Provision with him, he will be in danger of Starving; and if he once do approach his Enemy, yet he doth not presently open his Store of Provision, but reserves it for his Retreat; which, he knows, must be through those Places already wasted by such a Multitude of Men and Beasts, that, like Locusts, have before pillaged all the Country. Then, indeed, the *Grand Seignior*'s Stores are opened, and some small Allowance given out daily to the *Janizaries*, and other Dependents of that Prince, enough to keep them alive, and that's all. As for others, it goes hard with them, unless they have made some Provision for themselves before-hand; and some of their Soldiers, especially the Horse, are so fore-sighted that, in Prospect of such Difficulties, they carry a led Horse along with them, with Viands and other things to support them, if need be. Upon this Horse they usually carry some Blankets, that they may spread abroad, as Tents, to defend them from Sun and Rain; also some other Cloaths to wear, and withal two or three Wicker Baskets, full of the best Flower they can get, with a small Pot for Butter, some Spice and Salt; with these, in case of Necessity, they kill their Hunger. They take out a few Spoonfuls of their Meal or Flower, and pour Water upon it; then they add a little Butter, and so seasoning it with Spice and Salt, they set it on the Fire, and when it boils, it swells so that it will fill a large Platter.

They eat of this twice or thrice a Day, as their Store holds out, but without eating Bread with it, unless they have brought some Biskets along with them: And with this thin Diet, for want of better, they can live a Month or two, till they come to richer Quarters. There are some of them who carry dried Beef, grounded to Powder, in a kind of Snap-sack; that's a more nutritive and choice Viand amongst them: And sometimes they eat Horse-Flesh, for in a vast Army a great many Horses must needs die, and if any of them be more fleshy than others, they make a great Feast for hungry Stomachs. And those who have thus lost their Horses, (for you must know that too) when the *Grand Seignior* or *Vizier* removes his Camp, stand in a row before him in the Way he is to march, with their Saddles on their Heads, signifying hereby the Loss of their Horses, and by that mute Sign begging Relief towards buying a new one; and their Prince gratifies them, at his Pleasure.

Thus the *Turks* surmount huge Difficulties in War, with a great deal of Patience, Sobriety and Parsimony, reserving themselves for more favourable Circumstances. But our *Christian* Soldiers carry it otherwise; they scorn homely Fare in their Camps; they must have dainty bits, forsooth, such as Thrushes, Black-birds, and banquetting Stuff. If they have not these they are ready to mutiny, as if they were famished; and if they have them, they are undone: Their own Intemperance kills them, if their Enemy spare their Lives.

When I compare the Difference between their Soldiers and ours, I stand amazed to think what will be the Event; for certainly their Soldiers must needs conquer, and ours must needs be vanquished; both cannot stand prosperously together: For on their side, there is a mighty, strong and wealthy Empire, great Armies, Experience in War, a veteran Soldiery, a long Series of Victories, Patience in Toil, Concord, Order, Discipline, Frugality and Vigilance. On our side, there is public Want, private Luxury, Strength weakened, Minds Discouraged, an unaccustomedness to Labour or Arms, Soldiers refractory, Commanders covetous, a Contempt of Discipline, Licentiousness, Rashness, Drunkenness, Gluttony; and, what is worst of all, they used to conquer, we to be conquered. Can any Man doubt, in this case, what the Event will be? 'Tis only the *Persian* stands between us and Ruin. The *Turks* would fain be upon us, but he keeps him back; his War with him affords us only a Respite, not a Deliverance: When he once makes Peace with him, he will bring all the Power of the East upon us, and how ready we are to receive him, I am afraid to speak. But to return from whence I digressed.

I told you before, that the *Turks* use to carry their Arms and Tents on Horse-Back to the War; but they are such as chiefly belong to the *Janizaries*, for the *Turks* are very careful to have their Army healthy, and fenced against the Weather; let him defend himself as well as he can against the Enemy, that's to his own Peril; but the Public takes care for his Health. Hence it is, that the *Turkish* Army is better cloathed than armed. They are afraid of Cold, as of their greatest Enemy; and therefore, even in Summer-time, they are treble-clothed, and their inmost Garment (call it a Waistcoat, or whatever you will,) is made of coarse Thread, which keeps them very warm. And, to defend them also against the Cold and Showers, Tents are carried about for them at the Public Charge; and every *Janizary* is allowed as much Space in the Tent as the Dimensions of his Body are; so that one Tent can hold twenty five or thirty *Janizaries*; and that thick Cloath, I speak of, is also supplied out of the public Store. When it is distributed among them, they take this Course, to prevent Quarrels; the Soldiers are ranged in the Night in Files, in a Place appointed for that purpose, and so many Cloaths are brought out of the Store as there are Soldiers, and every one takes his Dole in the Dark; so that, if it be better or worse, he has no cause to complain. And, for the same Reason, their Pay is weighed out, not told, to them, lest any one should say, he was forced to receive light or clipt Money; nor do they stay till the very Pay-day, but receive it the Day before. The Arms that are carried are chiefly for the use of the Horse, called *Spahi's*; for the *Janizaries* do usually fight on Foot with Musquets, at a Distance, and therefore, when an Enemy is near, and a Battle expected, the Armour is produced; but usually such as is of an old Make, and are part of the Spoils obtained from former Fights and Victories: These are distributed among the Horse; their other Armour is but a light Buckler. You may easily think, how odly such Armour will fit on a Man which is given out so hastily. One's Breast-plate is too narrow; another Man's Helmet is too loose; another Coat of Mail is too heavy for him to bear. Every Piece hath some Fault or other; and yet they must not complain: They count it Cowardly so to do; for they resolve to fight, be their Arms what they will, so great Confidence have they in their Victories, and in the frequent Use of their Arms. Hence it is also, that they put their old Foot on Horse-service, which they were not used to before; for an experienced Soldier (they say) will do valiantly, either on Horse or Foot-service. In my Judgment, the *Old Romans* were of the same Mind, and especially *Julius Cæsar*, who was wont to say, *That his Soldiers would fight well, even though they were perfumed*; for when he horsed the ten Legions, upon a Conference he was to have with *Ariovistus*, what was his Intent, think we? but that they should fight on Horse-back, if there had been need, though they were used to Foot-service before; and we know amongst the *Romans*, their Foot-service was quite another thing from Horse-service. But if you say, *Cæsar*'s Design was only to horse his Men for Carriage, but to make use of their Service on Foot, certainly he had run a great Hazard thereby, if when *Ariovistus*'s choice Horse were within a Stone's Call of the *Romans*, and might have fallen upon them, the Legion was then to dismount their Horses, to be disposed of, and ranged into a *Foot-Tertia*, or Brigade, in an instant: With us, this would seem very absurd. However it be, this is certain, that experienced Soldiers will manage a Fight after a different Order than we do; so the *Romans* did of old, and so the *Turks* do at this Day, with too good Success. So much for that Subject.

I return, further to acquaint you, how indulgent the *Turks* are to all irrational Animals. 'Tis true, a Dog is counted an obscene and nasty Creature by them, and therefore they will not harbour him in their Houses; but they nourish a Cat as a chaster and modester Creature, in their Judgments. This Custom they received from *Mahomet*, their Law-giver, who was so much in love with a Cat, that, when one of them fell asleep upon his Sleeve, as he was reading at a Table, and the time of his Devotion drew near, he caused his Sleeve to be cut off, that he might not awake the Cat by his going to the Mosque.

HOWEVER, though the *Turks* have so ill an opinion of Dogs, that they wander up and down the City of *Constantinople*, and have no certain Masters, so that they are Keepers of Streets and Lanes, rather than of any certain House, and they live upon the Offal which is cast out of their Houses; yet, if they see any Bitch great with young, in their Neighbourhood, they give it Bones, and some Relicks of their Table: This they count an office of Pity amongst them. When, on this Account, I blamed them for performing such Offices to a *Brute*, which they would hardly do to a *Man*, though a reasonable Creature, like themselves, and to be sure, not to a *Christian*; their Answer was, that God had given Reason to Man, as a Fence against all Perils, and yet he did abuse it, so that if any Inconvenience or Trouble happened to him, it was his own Fault, and therefore he deserved less Pity: But God had bestowed no Boon on Brutes, but some natural Notions and Appetites, which of Necessity they must obey; and therefore they were to be relieved by Man's Help and Commiseration; and for this Reason they take it very ill, if any brute Creature be put to Torment at his Death, or that Men should take any Pleasure in tormenting them. This had like to cost a *Venetian* Goldsmith, that lived here, very dear, of late. The Story is worth telling. This Goldsmith did delight in the art of Fowling, and among other Birds, he once took one about the bigness of a Cuckow, and almost of the same Colour; he had no great Beak, but his Jaws were so wide and large, that, when they stretch'd asunder, they did gape most prodigiously, so that a Man's Fist might be thrust into them. The Man wondering at this strange kind of Bird, caus'd him to be fastened to the upper Lintel of his Gate, with his Wings spread abroad, and his Jaws so extended with a Stick, that he gaped hideously. The *Turks* came often by his Door, stood still, and looked upon it; but when they saw the Bird did move, and was alive, then taking Pity on it, *Out!* they cried, *What an abominable thing is this, that an harmless Bird should be so tormented?* Whereupon, out they call the Man of the House, and drag him presently, by Head and Shoulders, to their criminal Judge, where Sentence was likely to be pronounced upon him, to be soundly bastinadoed; but the *Bailo* of *Venice* (so they call their Ambassadors or Residents there) hearing of the Matter, sent presently one of his Servants to demand the Man, and the *Turkish Cadi* was so merciful as to let him go; but many of the *Turks* grumbled at his Freedom. Thus the poor Goldsmith scaped a Scouring: I laughed heartily at the Story, for he told it me himself, as coming often to my House, and in what a terrible Fright he was in for the time; and, to oblige me the more, he brought me the Bird to look upon. 'Tis of the same Form, as I lately described; it flies about in the Night, and (as they say) will suck Milch-Kine, so that I am apt to believe 'tis the Goat-Sucker of the Ancients. Such Commiseration do the *Turks* use towards all sorts of brute Animals, especially those of the winged Kind.

OVER against my Lodgings there is a tall *Plane-tree,* whose spreading Boughs make a delightsome Shade; under that Tree, sometimes Fowlers sit with abundance of such Birds to sell in Cages. You shall have the *Turks* buy several of these Birds for a small Matter; and when they have bought them, they'll let them fly out of their Hands. The Bird presently flies up to the Tree; there she picks her Feathers, and cleanseth them from the Filth contracted in the Cage, and then she spreads abroad her Wings, and chirps. The *Turks* that bought them, say, don't you hear how glad this Bird is, and how he gives me Thanks for his Liberty?

IF this be so, you'll say, What! are the *Turks* such *Pythagoreans,* that they count all Brutes sacred, and will eat none of their Flesh? I lay not so; but, on the contrary, they'll eat any Flesh set before them, either boil'd or roasted; only they count Mutton the properest Meat, because Sheep are made for the Shambles, as they say; yet they would not have Men to make a Sport at killing of them, as if they rejoyced in their Torment. Some of them will by no means be persuaded to kill small Birds which sing in their Fields and Woods; nay, they think it some Injury done them, to restrain their Liberty by caging them up. But all *Turks* are not of that Mind; some of them keep *Nightingales* in their Houses, for the Melodiousness of their Tunes, and in Spring-time they let them out to hire, to sing. I knew some, that carried *Linnets* about, so well instructed, that if a Man shew'd them a piece of Money out of his Chamber, though it were at a great distance from them, yet they would fly up to fetch it; and if the Man would not let it go, they would sit upon his Hand, and so accompany him from one Room to another, still pulling at the Money; and when they had got it, as if they remembred their Errand on which they were sent, when their Master whistled to them in the High-way, down they would fly to him again; and, as a Reward for the Money in their Bills, he would give them a little Hempseed. But I shall proceed no further in such Stories as these, lest you should think me a second *Pliny*, or an *Ælian*, and that I were designing to write an History of Animals.

I preceed then to other Matters, and shall give you an Example of the Chastity of *Turkish* Women. The *Turks* take more Pains to have their Wives modest, than any other Nation; and, therefore, they ordinarily keep them close up at home, and hardly suffer them to see the Sun; but if any necessity calls them abroad, they go so hooded and veil'd, as if they were Hobgoblins or Ghosts. 'Tis true, they can see Men through their Veils or Hoods, but no part of their Bodies is open to Man's View; for they have this Tradition among them, that it is impossible for a Man to look on a Woman, especially if she be young and handsome, without desiring to enjoy her; and by that Desire the Mind is excited, and therefore they keep them all covered. Their own Brothers have Liberty to see them; but their Husband's Brothers have not the same Permission. The nobler and richer sort, when they marry, do it with this Condition, that their Wives shall never set a Foot out of Door; and no Person living, either Male or Female, be the Cause what it will, shall ever have leave to see them; no, not their nearest Alliance in Blood, except only the Father and Mother, who, at *Easter*, (their *Bairam*) are permitted to see their Daughter; and, in lieu of this Strictness, if the Wife have Parents of the better sort, and she bring her Husband a large Dowry, the Husband, on his part promiseth, that he will never have any Concubines, but will keep to her alone.

In other Cases, the *Turks* have as many Concubines as they will, besides their lawful Wives; and the Children of both are equally respected, and have as much Privilege one as the other. Their Concubines they either buy, or take them in War, and, when they are weary of them, may sell them in the open Market; only if they have Children by them, then they obtain their Liberty. This made *Roxolana* stand upon her Terms with *Solyman*, in having brought him forth a Son, when she was a Slave, and thereby obtain'd Manumission. Hereupon she refused to submit to his Will any longer, unless he married her; which he, doting for Love, wou'd do, against the Custom of the *Ottoman* Princes.

A lawful Wife, with them, differs from a Concubine, only upon the account of her Dowry, which a lawful Wife hath, but a Concubine hath not. And when once her Dowry is assigned her, then she is a Mistress; Governess of the House, and all the other Women under her. And yet the Husband hath leave to lie with which of them he pleases at his Choice; and when he makes known his Pleasure to his Wife, she bids the Maid of his desires prepare herself for his Bed; and she obeys; perhaps, more joyfully than her Mistress commands her. Only *Friday* Night, which is their *Sabbath*, the Wife claims as her due, and she thinks herself wrong'd, if her Husband defraud her thereof; other Nights he may lie with which of his Slaves he pleases.

Divorces are made among them for many Causes, which Men easily pretend; and when a Wife is divorced, her Dowry is restored, unless she be put away on a dishonest Account: But Women have but few; to instance some among those few, this is one, if their Husband do not allow them due Maintenance; and if they offer to abuse them against Nature, (a Crime usual among them) then the Wife goes to the Judge, and tells him, she can no longer endure to live with her Husband; when he asks the Cause, they say nothing, but pull off their Shoe from their Feet, and turn it up and down, which is a Sign among them of the unlawful use of Copulation. The greatest sort among them, that have abundance of Women, set *Eunuchs* to guard them, not such as have only their Stones taken out, but such whose Yards are also impaired; because other wise they think, such as have lost their Stones only, may desire the use of a Woman, tho' not for Generation, yet for Pleasure. The great Men also have Baths at their own Houses, wherein they and their Women do wash; but the meaner sort use public Baths.

A *Turk* hates bodily Filthiness and Nastiness, worse than Soul-Defilement; and, therefore, they wash very often, and they never ease themselves, by going to Stool, but they carry Water with them for their Posteriors. But ordinarily the Women bathe by themselves, Bond and Free together; so that you shall many times see young Maids, exceeding beautiful, gathered from all Parts of the World, exposed Naked to the view of other Women, who thereupon fall in Love with them, as young Men do with us, at the sight of Virgins.

By this you may guess, what the strict Watch over Females comes to, and that it is not enough to avoid the Company of an adulterous Man, for the *Females* burn in Love one towards another; and the Pandaresses to such refined Loves are the Baths; and, therefore, some *Turks* will deny their Wives the use of their public Baths, but they cannot do it altogether, because their Law allows them. But these Offences happen among the ordinary sort; the richer sort of Persons have Baths at home, as I told you before.

It happened one time, that at the public Baths for Women, an old Woman fell in Love with a Girl, the Daughter of a poor Man, a Citizen of *Constantinople*; and, when neither by wooing nor flattering her, she could obtain that of her which her mad Affection aim'd at, she attempted to perform an Exploit almost incredible; she feign'd herself to be a Man, changed her Habit, hired an House near the Maid's Father, and pretended she was one of the *Chiauxes* of the *Grand Seignior*; and thus, by reason of his Neighbourhood, she insinuated herself into the Man's Acquaintance, and after some time, acquaints him with the desire of his Daughter. In short, he being a Man in such a prosperous Condition, the Matter was agreed on, a Portion was settled, such as they were able to give, and a Day appointed for the Marriage; when the Ceremonies were over, and this doughty Bridegroom went into the Bride-chamber to his Spouse; after some Discourse, and plucking off her Headgeer, she was found to be a Woman. Whereupon the Maid runs out, and calls up her Parents, who soon found that they had married her, not to a *Man*, but a *Woman*: Whereupon, they carried the supposed Man, the next day, to the General of the *Janizaries*, who, in the Absence of the *Grand Seignior*, was Governor of the City. When she was brought before him, he chide her soundly for her beastly

Love; what, says he, are you not asham'd, an old Beldam as you are, to attempt so notorious a Bestiality, and so filthy a Fact?

Away, Sir, says she! You do not know the Force of Love, and God grant you never may. At this absurd Reply, the Governor could scarce forbear Laughter, but commanded her, presently, to be pack'd away and drown'd in the Deep; such was the unfortunate Issue of her wild Amours. For you must know, that the *Turks* make no noise when *secret* Offences are committed by them, that they may not open the Mouths of Scandal and Reproach; but *open* and *manifest* ones they punish most severely. I am afraid the Relation of that dismal Example hath grated your Ears. I shall, therefore, now endeavour to make you amends, by acquainting you with a pleasant Story, which, I believe, will go near to make you smile. 'Tis this.

Upon the Account of the Troubles in *Hungary*, there came lately a Messenger to me, with an Express from my Master, the Emperor. The *Bashaws* would not let him bring his Letters directly to me, as they were wont to be brought, but they carried him first into the *Divan*. The Reason of this their unusual Procedure, was, because they would fain know what *Cæsar*'s Letters did contain, before they were delivered, in regard they suspected I dealt not faithfully with them, in communicating my Master's Sense, but that I suppressed some of his Concessions. The Messenger was cunning enough for them; for, having some inkling of the Matter beforehand, he hid *Cæsar*'s Letters, and only shew'd them those that were directed to me, from some particular Friends. Their interpreter, *Ebrahim*, a *Polander* by Birth, had acquainted them before, that the Letters, that brought any secret Commands to me, were not written in an ordinary Character, but in a new kind of Marks, called *Cyphers*. As they were searching all my Letters, at last they light upon One, that was wrote to me by a Friend of mine, a Secretary of *Burgundy*. *Ebrahim* saw, through the thinness of the Paper wherein 'twas writ, some shining Letters, which were not of an ordinary sort. O! says he, now I have found it out; don't you meddle with any of the rest of the Packet, for here's the Secrecy in this. Whereupon the *Bashaws* commanded him to open, read, and interpret it to them, and they all stood listning to hear the News; but *Ebrahim* told them plainly, that he could not read one Letter of it. That's strange, says the *Bashaws*; what, did you never learn the *Christian* Alphabet; or have you forgot it? Says *Ebrahim*, this sort of Character is only known to those who are Secretaries to Princes: They did not well understand him; but however, say they, if it be so, why dost thou not make haste to the Secretary of the *Bailo* of *Venice*, or of *Florence*? *Ebrahim* presently makes haste to them, and shews them the Letters; (they were writ in might such a Character that a Child ten Years old have read them;) but both those Secretaries, when they saw the Letter was superscrib'd to me, threw it back again before they had well look'd upon it; alledging, in Excuse, that such kind of Letters could be read by none, unless by him who had another Cypher to unfold them. This was all the Answer *Ebrahim* could get of them. Upon his Return to the *Bashaws* therewith, they could not tell what in the World to do: At last, starts up one (I could not tell his Name) saying, there is a Patriarch in Town, and old Man, and a *Christian*, and, besides, a great Scholar; if any Man can read these Letters, it must be he. When they came to the Patriarch, he told them, he could not read a Tittle of them, for they were not writ in *Greek*, *Latin*, *Hebrew* or *Chaldee*. Thus they were disappointed there also. At last, *Haly Bassa* runs to *Rustan* (otherwise a Man not ready to jest) and says to him *Cardassi* (Brother in *Turkish*), I remember, I had once a Servant, an *Italian*, who was skilled in all Letters and Tongues, I do not question but he could have read the Letter; but, alas! he is lately dead. At last, they being at a stand what to do, thought it best to send the Letters, which they could make no use of, to me. I knew all the Matter by *Ebrahim* beforehand, (neither could it be kept secret); whereupon I began to stamp and fret that they had intercepted my Letters against the Law of Nations, and in Contempt of *Cæsar* who sent them; and, withal, I bid *Ebrahim* stay, and to Morrow he should see that Letter translated for the *Bashaws*. The next day, when *Ebrahim* appeared in the *Divan*, they asked of him, whether I could read those Letters? Read them, says he! as easily as his own Name; and thereupon he produced some of them translated before them, *viz.* what I had a mind to discover. Whereupon, says *Rustan*, this Ambassador is but a young Man, and yet we see he can understand what the old Patriarch could not so much as read; without doubt, if he live to be old, he will prove a very *Nonsuch* of a Man. For that reason it was, or perhaps some other, that a while after, having Conference with *Rustan* about our Affairs, he treated me more familiarly than he used to do, (which was a rare thing in him) and at last he ask'd me, why I would not turn to their Religion, and to the true Worship of God? If I would do so, he promised me great Honour and a large Reward from their Emperor *Solyman*. I told him, I was resolved to continue in that Religion, wherein I was born, and which my Master, *Cæsar*, did profess. Be it so, replied he; but what then will become of your Soul? I subjoined, I hope well for that too; whereupon he, after a little Pause, broke forth into these Words. 'Tis true, indeed, and I am almost of your Mind, that they who live holy and modest Lives in this present World, shall obtain eternal Life in the next, be they of what Religion they will. That's an Heresy, that some of the *Turks* have taken up, neither is *Rustan* thought to be a true *Mussulman* in all Points. The *Turks* thinks it a Duty, and a work of Piety in them, to persuade a *Christian* they have any good Opinion of, to their Religion; for then they think, they shall save a Soul from Destruction, and that they count a great Honour to themselves, and the greatest Charity they can do another Man, to make him a Convert to their Religion.

I shall now acquaint you with the Effects of another Conference I had with *Rustan*, whereby you may see what daily Feuds are between the *Turks* and *Persians*, upon the account of Religion. He ask'd me, one time, whether the War did continue between *Spain* and *France*? I told him, it did. 'Tis strange, says he, that they should fall out that are of one and the same Religion: I replied, 'tis no otherwise between those two Princes, than 'tis betwixt *you* and the *Persians*. The Dispute is not about Religion, but about civil Right; Provinces, Cities and Kingdoms, which both lay claim to. You are quite mistaken, says *Rustan*, we are not of the same Religion with the *Persians*, but do count them a more Profane and *Heathenish* sort of People than you *Christians* are. But to return to the Affairs of *Hungary*.

Since my last Return to *Constantinople*, Matters in *Hungary* have received a very great Alteration, it would be too tedious to describe them particularly; and, besides, it were not conducive to my Design. *Isabella*, Wife to King *John*, is returned into *Transilvania*, together with her Son, having refused the Transactions and broken the League made with the Emperor *Ferdinand*; and the *Transilvanians*, terrified by the *Turkish* Arms, have again submitted their Necks to the old *Ottoman* Yoke. Matters succeeding thus prosperously with the *Turks*, they are not therewith contented, but grasp at all *Hungary* too; and, besides other Places, they resolved to besiege *Sigeth*, which signifies in the *Hungarian* Language, an *Island*, or Place naturally very strongly situated. And for this purpose they chose a General, who, upon the account of the Prosperity of his Arms in former times, created great Confidence in his own Men, and struck as much Terror into his Enemy: His Name was *Haly Bassa*, an *Epirot*, who had had good Success in *Hungary* before, and especially in the Battel, wherein he overthrew *Sforza Palavicino*, and the Bishop of Five Churches. He was sent for from the utmost Bounds of the *Turkish* Empire towards *Persia*, and came with great Expectation to *Constantinople*: My Collegues were yet here with me, pressing for a Dismission. 'Twas the pleasure of the *Bashaws* that we should see him, in regard we counted him, as they thought, the very Thunder-bolt of War.

When we came to him, he received us courteously, and made a great Harangue to this purpose: That, "we should study Peace, and rather than suffer *Hungary* to be wasted with Fire and Sword, we should accept those Conditions, which the *Grand Seignior* had offered us." We answered him, that "we desired nothing more than Peace; provided it might be had upon tolerable Conditions; but those which they offered, were against the Honour and Dignity of our Master." Thus we took our leaves, after he had treated us with a Cup of Water diluted with Sugar. This *Haly* was an Eunuch, but the Constitution of his Body did seem to add to the vigour of his Mind: He was low of Stature, bloted in his Body, of a Bay-coloured Countenance, a sour Look, frowning Eyes, broad Shoulders and sticking up, between which stood his Head, as in a Valley. Two Teeth were prominent in his Mouth, like Boar's Tusks, his Voice hoarse; in a Word, he was the Fourth Fury.

THE Day after he makes great Preparation for his Expedition into *Hungary*; where having spent some Time to provide Materials, he at last marches against *Sigeth*, and beats off those which were repairing *Babock*, a Castle of *Cæsar*'s; but *Cæsar*, being acquainted long before with his Design, lends *Ferdinand*, one of his three Sons, a young Man, yet comparable, for greatness of Mind, to any of the old Generals, to oppose the Torrent of *Haly Bassa*'s Force, and by his Valour to retrieve Affairs in *Hungary*: He had no great Forces with him, but with a select Body of Horse he faces *Haly*'s Army; the *Turks* that were present, related to me, that 'twas a goodly Sight to behold the Splendor, Order and Boldness of those Forces. *Haly*, being naturally of a fierce Disposition, and having a far greater Army, was even mad to think that a handful of *Christians* should dare to look him in the Face.

THERE was a moorish Piece of Ground between both Armies, which could not be passed without great Danger; *Ferdinand* had no need to pass it, for his Design was only to relieve *Sigeth*, and to raise the Siege: But *Haly Bassa*, was not in the same Circumstances; for, unless he would make a base and unhandsome Retreat (as the Event afterwards shewed) 'twas altogether necessary for him to do it; So that he, seeing to what Straits he was brought, resolved to put all upon hazard, and accordingly he bent his Bridle, to turn his Horse towards that inconvenient Place; when, behold! one of the *Sanziacks*, that was near him, whose Name I remember not, taking Notice of the extream Danger he was running into, leap'd from his Horse, and taking the *Bashaw*'s Horse by the Bridle, *Sultan*, says he (for so the *Turks* call the great Dignitaries among them) *Here you see into what a Jeopardy you were like to cast both yourself and your whole Army; you don't consider what an incommodious Place this Marish is: The* Christians *are ready on the other side with Arms in Hand and Courage in their Hearts, to receive us, when we are half drowned and half covered with Mud; and thus they in good Order will assault us, being disordered and out of our Ranks, and will make use of all our Imprudence, to obtain a most assured Victory over us: Nay, rather moderate your Anger, and return to yourself and reserve so many brave Men, with yourself for the Service of your Prince, and for better Times.* Upon this Speech, *Haly*, as if he had recollected himself, drew back; and there was not any *Turk* amongst them, but was forced to confess, that the whole Army was sav'd by the Advice of that *Sanziack*.

When this matter was carried to *Constantinople*, though the *Vizier* and the Chief *Bashaws* could not deny the Thing, yet they thought it dangerous to suffer the Example of so audacious a Fact in the *Sanziack* to pass unpunished: 'Tis true, they did mutteringly commend both his Fidelity and his Prudence; yet to suffer Disobedience to a superior Officer to pass without due Punishment, they thought it a dangerous Case in Military Discipline, so that he was called back to *Constantinople*, and there was cashiered for a Time; and when this Offence was sufficiently punished, as they thought, they bestowed upon him as good a Command; so that every Body saw his Punishment was inflicted rather for the preservation of the Discipline of War, than for any dire Merit of his Offence.

Haly, a while after, having lost a great Part of his Army, by the Charges and Ambuscades of the *Hungarians*, made an ignoble and shameful Retreat to *Buda*, where for very Grief he breathed out his hateful Soul.

But Arch-duke *Ferdinand*, on the other side, returned to *Ferdinand* his Father, with the deserved Laurel of Victory, having performed an Exploit, not only of great Advantage for the present, but of much greater Benefit to future Ages, by the Example it gave; for hereby he made the *Turks* to know that if they proceeded on to press upon *Cæsar*, he wanted neither able Soldiers, nor expert Commanders to chastise their Insolency.

Yet the *Turks* of those Borders did not carry it with any great Modesty; for, while *Haly* was yet encamped at *Sigeth*, our Men had scaled the Walls of *Gran*, and taken the City, having a Castle near it of the same Name, where they got a great deal of Booty, and carried away the Inhabitants, being mostly Women and Children.

A Messenger was sent immediately to *Haly*, to acquaint him of the Loss; who coming into his Presence, by the very Consternation of his Countenance portended some great Mischief to have happened to them. The *Bassa* presently asked him, how Things went? and what was the Cause of his great Fear? *Sir*, says he, *the Enemy hath taken and plundered* Gran; *which great Blow occasions my Grief. A Blow, Fool*, says the *Bassa*! *tell me of a Blow when I have lost my Genitals* (to which he pointed with his Hand) *that shew me to be a Man.* Thus did he scoff at the Consternation of the Messenger, not without the Laughter of the By-standers, and undervalued the Loss of *Gran*, which was easily recoverable.

Moreover, in *Croatia* and the adjoyning Countries, several Inroads were made by both Parties, and each side did alternately suffer for their over-boldness and supine Security. Let me give you an Instance, which, as it gave me joy, will not, I dare say, be unpleasant, to you to hear of. It happened, indeed, some what before the Passage at *Sigeth* lately mentioned; but in Writing an Epistle, I do not strictly observe the Order of Time.

News was brought to *Rustan*, from those Parts, that a certain Confident of his, whom he highly esteemed, and called Cousin, had fallen upon a Party of *Christians*, as they were celebrating a Wedding, and being at a sufficient Distance, as they thought, from the *Turks*, counted themselves secure; when behold this bold and unwelcome Guest, with Armed Forces, came in upon them, spoiled their Mirth, slew some, and took some Prisoners, among whom was the unfortunate Bridegroom, with his un-bedded Spouse: *Rustan* did much rejoyce at this Exploit, and in all Companies highly commended the Stratagem of his Kinsman, for performing it.

A pitiful Case, you will say, rather to be lamented than related: But these are the Tragical Sports of insolent Fortune; yet Revenge followed him at the Heels, *Rustan*'s Laughter was soon turned to Sadness: For a little while after one of the *Deli's*, or mad Sparks, a sort of furious Horsemen among the *Turks*, so called by their outragious Boldness, came post to him out of *Dalmatia*, and told him, that a parcel of *Turks* had made an Excursion into the Enemies Country, and had got great Booty, but seting no bounds to their Avarice, they, at last were encountered with a Party of *Christians*, *Dragoons* or *Musketeers*, who totally routed them, slew many *Sanziacks*, and among them his *Achillean* Cousin, lately so much extolled by him. This sad News made *Rustan* burst out into Tears, so that his fit of Laughter was justly requited. But hearken to the close of the Story, which is not unpleasant: When this *Dalmatian* Trooper, who brought the News, was asked by the *Bassa*, in the *Divan*, How many were there of you? He answered, above two thousand five hundred: And how many of the *Christians*? I think, says he, they were not above five hundred, unless there were more of them in ambush, as we suspected. Fie for Shame, said the fretting *Bassas*! what! a regular Army of *Mussulmans* (so they call the Men of their own Religion) to be beaten by so small a handful of *Christians*! You are goodly Warriors indeed! fit to eat the *Sultan*'s Bread, are, you not? The blunt Fellow, nothing dismay'd, replied, you are quit beside the Cushion; did I not tell you that we were beaten by Musketeers? 'Twas the Fire defeated us, not the Valour of our Enemies. We had come off Conquerors, if we had contested by Valour only; but who can fight against Fire, the fiercest of Elements? and what Mortal can stand, if the very Elements fight against him? This bold Answer of his, being as saucily pronounced, made the By-standers ready to burst out into a Laughter, though on this sad occasion to them.

This Matter did very much raise my Spirits, which were quite sunk at the Remembrance of the former Mis-hap of the Marriage-Feast. This Story informs us, that our Pistols and Carbines, which are used on Horseback, are a great Terror to the *Turks*, as I hear they are to the *Persians* also; for once, there was a Fellow that persuaded *Rustan*, when he accompanied his Prince in a War against *Persia*, to arm two hundred Horse of his Domesticks with Pistols: For those, said he, will be terrible to our Enemy, and will also do great execution upon them. *Rustan* hearkned to his Counsel, and furnished out a Party, as advised; but, before they had marched half way, their Carbines or Pistols were ever now and then out of Order; one thing or other was broke or lost, and scarce any Body could mend them: Hereupon this Party was useless. The *Turks* were also against this Armature, because it was slovenly (the *Turks*, you must know, are much for cleanliness in War); for the Troopers Hands were black and sooty, their Cloaths full of Spots, and their Case-boxes that hung by their Sides made them ridiculous to their Fellow-Soldiers, who therefore jeered them, with the Title *Medicamentarii*, or *Mountebank Soldiers*; hereupon they apply themselves to *Rustan*, complaining of this broken, useless Armour, which could do no Service against an Enemy, and entreating to have their usual Weapons again, their Bows and Arrows; which, are readily granted them.

THE mention I made a while ago of things acted in the Confines of *Hungary*, gives me occasion to tell you, what the *Turks* think of Duels, which amongst *Christians* is accounted a singular Proof of personal Valour. There was one *Arslambeg,* a *Sanziack,* that lived in the Frontiers of *Hungary,* who was very much famed for a robust Person; he was very expert at the Bow; no Man brandished his Sword with more Strength, or was more terrible to his Enemy. Not far from him there dwelt one *Uliber,* a *Sanziack* also, who was emulous of the same Praise; and this Emulation (heighten'd, perhaps, by other Motives) at length occasioned Hatred and many bloody Combats between them. It happened thus, *Uliber* was sent for to *Constantinople*; upon what occasion I know not. When he came thither, and the *Bashaws* had asked many Questions of him, in the *Divan,* concerning other Matters, at last they demanded how he and *Arslambeg* (*Arsla* signifies a Lion in *Turkey*) came to fall out? Hereupon he makes a long Narration of the Grudges between them, with their Causes and Progress; and to put a fairer Gloss on his own Cause, he added, that once *Arslambeg* had laid an Ambush, and wounded him treacherously: And that, said he, he needed not have done, if he would have shewed himself worthy the Name he bears; for I have often challenged him to fight Hand to Hand, and never shun'd to meet him in the Field. The *Bashaws,* much offended, thus replied, *How durst thou challenge thy Fellow-Soldier to a Duel? What, was there never a* Christian *to fight with? Do not both of you eat your Emperor's Bread? And yet, forsooth, you must go about to take away one another's Lives! What Precedent had you for this? Don't you know, that whoever of the two had died, the Emperor had lost a Subject?* Whereupon, by their Command, he was haled to Prison, where he lay pining many Months, and was, at last, with Difficulty, released; yet with the loss of his Reputation.

AMONG us *Christians,* many who have never come in sight of a public Enemy, draw their Swords upon one another, and think it a brave and honourable Thing. What shall a Man do in such a Case, when Vice usurps the seat of Virtue, and that which deserves Punishment, is counted noble and glorious? But to return, I know you are inquisitive, and therefore give me leave to acquaint you with the public Entrance, which the King of *Cholchos* made into this City. His Kingdom is by the River *Phasis,* in a Creek or Bay of the *Euxine* Sea, not far from Mount *Caucasus.* His Name is *Dadianus,* a Man of a tall Stature and grateful Countenance, but of a rough-hew'n Disposition, as some say. He came with a great Train, but in a very Thread-bare, and old-fashion'd Garb. The *Italians*, at this Day, call the *Colchians Mingrelians*: They are some of that People, inhabiting between the *Caspian Gates*, (called by the *Turks, Demit capi*, i. e. *Iron Gates*,) and the *Potic* and *Hyrcanian*-Seas: They are at this Day called *Georgians*; whether from that sort of Christian Religion, which they profess, or whether that be their ancient Name (which seems most probable,) is not fully determined. The *Albanians* and *Iberians* are reckoned a Part of them. The Cause of his coming is uncertain: Some say, he was sent for by the *Turk*; for, when he makes Wars upon the *Persian*, if the *Colchians* and the People of that Tract join with him, they may give him notable Assistance. But the vulgar and more credible Opinion was, that he came to desire the Assistance of some Gallies against his Neighbour, the *Iberian*, who had slain his Father; which if he could obtain, then he would become Tributary to the *Sultan*. For, you must know, that there is an old and inveterate Hatred between the *Colchians* and the *Iberians*. Once there were some Overtures of Accommodation between them, and a Conference was had thereupon, between great Numbers of both Nations. At this Meeting, they began, first, to try who should be the greatest Drinkers; in which Contest, the *Colchians*, fell fast asleep. The treacherous *Iberians* made use of this Opportunity, and hurried away honest *Dadianus* as yet snoring, into a Chariot, and shut him up Prisoner in a high Tower, as if he had been lawful Prize taken in War. To revenge this Injury, and to recover their King, the *Colchians* levied an Army of 30,000 Men, who were commanded by the Wife of the captive King, a Woman of great Spirit, and not unskill'd in Horsemanship, or handling of Arms. The Commanders, in this Army, wore huge and unwieldy Coats of Mail, and were also armed with Swords and Spears pointed with Iron. They had also amongst them, a party of Musketeers, a strange sight in that Country. As for the common Soldiers, they had no Arms, but Arrows, or Stakes burnt at one end, or great wooden Clubs. Thus they rode on Horseback, without Saddle or other Furnture.

THIS rude and discomposed Multitude, drew near to the Place where their King was in Custody, but were soon terrified with the Discharge of a few Guns from the Castle, and ran back a full Mile; but then taking Heart, on they came again, but were repulsed with the like Noise as before. *Dadianus*, perceiving help so near, cut his Bedcloaths into a kind of Ropes, and so let himself down by Night, through his Window, and fled to his own People.

This Stratagem of their King, and the successful Issue of it, is highly praised by that People, even to this very day.

The Country of *Colchis* abounds with all sorts of Fruits, growing almost naturally, except Bread-Corn, Wheat and Barley; and these Grains would grow there also, if due Tillage were used about them: But the People are very idle, they only sow Millet at random, which yields such an Encrease, that one Crop serves them for two Years; their chief Subsistence is thereon, neither desire they any other Corn. Their Vines grow at the foot of high Trees, and mounting up to their Boughs, yield them much Wine, and pretty good. These Vines last for many Years. Their Bees, like themselves, live in the Woods, and supply them with Wax and Honey; all the Pains they take, is, to find them out. The same Woods yield them plenty of Venison; as for Pheasants and Partridges, they abound all over the Country. A great proof of the Fertility of their Land, are their Melons, which, besides their extraordinary Sweetness, do oft grow three Foot long.

As for coin'd Silver, they have little or none, and of Gold less; few of them know what it is: So that they may seem a very happy People, who are without so great a Temptation to Mischief. And yet I think few of us do envy them this Happiness, because none can grow rich among them; yet they have that value for Silver, that when they receive any in Traffick with Foreigners, as some of them must needs do, they transfer it all to he use of their Temples, for making Crucifixes, Chalices and such like Ornaments, which sometimes their King, on pretence of Public Necessity, doth seize upon, and amass it all to his own use.

Their only way of Commerce among themselves is by exchange of Wares. If one have overmuch of a Commodity, he brings it to Market, and receives what he wants in Exchange; so that there is no need of Money, their Commerce is by bartering of Commodities.

They pay also their Tribute to their King in the Products of the Earth; they supply him with all Necessaries largely, both for Meat, Drink, and Apparel, for maintaining of his Houshold, and is reward the Deserving. And, indeed, he hath an unexhausted Revenue, not only from Tenths, and settled Customs, but from those Gifts which are daily bellowed upon him; and yet he is as liberal in bellowing them, as he is ready to receive them.

His Palace is, as a public Granary, stored with all manner of Provisions, which are disposed to all that need, out of his royal Bounty; especially if that Year's Harvest hath disappointed the Husbandman. The Custom is, that if any Merchant come with his Ship thither, he makes a Present to the King, either small or great, nothing is refused, and the King bestows a Banquet on them ashore. The manner is thus.

There is a large Building, on both sides of which are the King's Stables, where a long Table is plac'd for the King; he himself fits at the upper end, and, at a moderate Distance, fit the rest. The Table is well furnished, especially with Venison, and with Wine enough; the largest Drinkers are the welcomest Guests. The Queen, with her female Attendants, hath a Table in the same Room, but apart by themselves; and then they junket freely without much regard to Modesty; they carry themselves like Anticks, fleering, nodding, tipping the Wink, like so many *Medea's*, if there were *Jasons* ready for them.

After Dinner, the King, with his Guests, goes a Hunting; and, in Woods, under the Shadow of large Trees, the common People divert themselves, and keep Holy-day in Drinking, Dancing and Singing. They hang their Fiddles on long Poles or Boards, and then striking them with a Stick, make Musick, and sing to it the Praise of their Mistresses, or of their valiant Men. Among their Heroes (unless I am misinformed) they often mention one *Rowland*; how he came into that Country I know not, unless he passed thither with *Godfrey* of *Bullogne*. They tell many prodigious Stories of this *Rowland*, as ridiculous and improbable as any Romance among us.

Whilst they are thus given to Idleness and Luxury, Dissoluteness must needs follow; and, to speak Truth, Chastity is a Virtue rarely found among them. The Husband will offer his own Wife or his Sister, to the Pleasure of a Stranger; and, if they can but thus please their Wives, they care for little else. Neither are their Daughters kept under any stricter Discipline. 'Tis hard to find a Damsel unvitiated among them; nay, some have born Children at ten Years old; and, if you scruple to believe it, because of the smallness of their Bodies, at your Request they will produce you an Infant, not much bigger than a large Frog. Whereas, otherwise, they are a tall and comely bodied People. But they are so void of all Civility and courteous Behaviour, that they think they pay you a great Compliment, if among other

Barbarities, when they meet you, they make a certain Sound from their Throats like Belching.

In one thing they shew a great Dexterity of Wit, and that is in Stealing. He that pilfers most neatly, is counted a brave Fellow; but he that does it bungingly, is esteemed a Dunce and a Blockhead, not worthy to live; and even his own Father or his Son, will sell or exchange him for a small Matter to Merchant-strangers, to be carried away they care not whither.

An *Italian* Merchant who had been in these Parts, told me, that a certain Priest of theirs, stole his Knife as he was in their Temple. He perceived the Theft, but dissembling it, gave him the Sheath also, that he might put up his stol'n Ware.

When they go into their Temples, they have some esteem for the Images of the Virgin *Mary*, of *Peter* and *Paul*, and other Saints; but their greatest Veneration is for the Image of St. *George* on Horseback. They fall down prostrate before it, kissing every part of it; even his Horse's Shoes. They say, he was a valiant Man, a great Warrior, that in a single Combat did openly fight Hand to Hand with the *Devil*, and either conquer'd, or, at least, foil'd him.

I'll acquaint you with one Passage more, which you cannot but stand amazed at. 'Tis this.

The Princes of the East are always presented with Gifts at any Audience. *Dadianus*, in compliance with this Custom, brought *Solyman* a Cup or Dish of Carbuncle, so bright and shining, that in a dark Night a Man might travel by the Light of it, as well as at Noon-day. I cannot believe it, you'll say: Nor do I: Neither can I be angry with you for suspending your Belief; but, whatever you and I do, let me tell you, there are enough that do believe it. The more judicious think it to be a small Goblet of *Carbuncle*, or *Granate*, which was lost in Shipwrack, when a certain Prince of *Persia* was flying from his Father to *Constantinople*, and driven, by a Tempest, to the *Colchian* Shore, where it was taken up. He brought also 20 white *Hawks*, called *Falcons*, there being Plenty of them in that Country of *Colchis*.

This is all I can inform you of, concerning the *Colchians* and their Manners; let me now proceed to answer your Demands concerning my self, and my own way of Living. I seldom go abroad, unless I receive Letters from my Master to be delivered at the Court; or, unless I am commanded to expostulate with the *Bashaws* concerning the Rapines and Cruelties of the *Turkish* Garrisons, which is ordinarily twice or thrice a Year. Perhaps, if I would desire leave to ride about the City with my Keeper, it would not be denied me: But I have no mind to be so much beholding to them; for I would have them think that the strictness of my Confinement or Imprisonment is not valued at all by me; and, to speak Truth, what Comfort can I have to ride up and down among a parcel of *Turks*, who will either slight, or else jeer and reproach me? No, I like the Country and the Champaign better than the City; especially that City which is so full of Ruins, and which retains nothing of its ancient Glory, besides its Situation. 'Tis true, it was once a Rival to *Rome* it self; but now, alas! it is shamefully inslaved; who can without Pity behold it? Who so hard-hearted, as not to be affected with the mutability of human Affairs? And who knows how near we are to the same Fate? I keep my self within my own Doors, conversing with my old Friends, I mean, my Books, in which is all my Delight. 'Tis true, for my Health's Sake, I have made a Bowling-Green, where, before Dinner, I use to play; and, after Dinner, I practise the *Turkish* Bow.

THE *Turks* are wondrous expert at shooting with the Bow; they accustom themselves to that Exercise from 7 or 8, to 18 or 20 Years of Age, and hereby their Arms grow stronger, and their Skill so great, that they will hit the smallest Mark with their Arrows. Their Bows are not much stronger, but for their shortness much handier than ours; they are not made of plain Wood, but of a String and Ox's Horn, fastened with much Glew and Flax. These sort of Bows, though never so strong, the *Turks*, who are used to the Sport, can easily draw even to their very Ear; and yet one that is not accustom'd thereto, though never so strong a Man, cannot draw to that height, so as to strike a piece of Money, set upright between the Bow and the String, in the Angle where it is put into the Notch.

THEY aim their Arrows so sure, that in a Fight they will hit a Man's very Eye, or any other Part they design to strike. In the place where they exercise, you may see them direct by their stroke so artificially, that 5 or 6 of their Arrows will stick round about the White in the Butt, (which is usually less than a Dollar) and yet not hurt or touch it. They stand not above 30 Foot from the Butt: In the Thumb of their Right Hand, they use Rings of Bone, on which the String lies, when they draw it; and with the Thumb of their Left Hand, they draw the Arrow by a knot bearing outwards; far otherwise than they do with us. Their Butt is made of a Bank of sandy, gravelly Earth, raised about four Foot high from the Ground, and strongly surrounded with Boards. But the *Bashaws*, and those that have great Families, train up their Servants in this Exercise, at their own Houses, where the more skilful teach the unexperienced. Some of these in their solemn *Bayram*, (for they also have their *Easter*) assemble themselves together in a great Plain about *Pera*, where sitting over-against one another cross-legg'd, as Taylors do with us, (for that is the manner of their sitting) they begin with Prayer (so the *Turks* begin all their Enterprizes) and then they strive, who shall shoot an Arrow farthest. The whole Contest is managed with a great deal of Decency and Silence, though the number of Spectators be very great. Their Bows are very short for this Exercise, and the shorter the better, so that they are hardly bendable, but by well-practised Persons: Their Arrows also are of a peculiar kind. He that conquers hath a Linnen-Handkerchief, such as we use to wipe off our Sweat, wrought with embroidered Needle-work, for his Reward; but his greatest Encouragement, is the Commendation and Renown he gets. 'Tis almost incredible how far they will shoot an Arrow; they mark the place, with a Stone, where the farthest Arrow, for that Year, was lodg'd. There are many such Stones in the Field, placed there Time out of Mind, which are farther than they are able to shoot now a-days, they say. These were the Marks of their Ancestor's Archery, whose Skill and Strength in Shooting, they acknowledge, they cannot reach to. In divers Streets and Cross-ways of the City of *Constantinople*, there are also such Sports, wherein not only Children and young Men, but even the graver sort do exercise themselves. There is one that takes care of the Butt, who waters it every Day, otherwise it would be so dry, that an Arrow (the *Turkish* Arrows being always blunt) would not stick therein. And he that thus oversees the Mark is very diligent to draw out and to cleanse the Arrows, and throw them back to the Archers, and he hath a Stipend from them sufficient to maintain him. The Front of the Butt is like a little Door, whence, perhaps, came the *Greek* Proverb; that, when a Man miss'd the Mark, he is said to shoot *extra januam*, besides the Door; for, I suppose, the *Greeks* used this way of Butting, and that the *Turks* borrowed it from them. I grant the use of the Bow is very ancient among the *Turks*; but that hinders not, but, when they conquered the *Grecian* Cities, they might still retain their way of butting and bounding their Arrows. For no Nation scruples to transfer the profitable Inventions of other Nations to themselves, as I might instance in *Great Ordnance*, and in *Muskets*, and other things, which, though not our Inventions, yet the *Turks* borrow their use of from us.

'Tis true, they could never yet be brought to the Printing of Books, nor to the setting up public Clocks. The Reasons are, that their Scripture (*i. e.*) *Alchoran*, would no longer be called Scripture, or Writing, if it were Printed, (that's their Fancy); and for Clocks, they suppose, that the Authority of their *Emraim*, and of their ancient Rites would be diminished, if they should permit the Use of them. In other Cases, they ascribe much to the ancient Institutions of other Nations, even almost to the prejudice of their own Religion. I speak of their Commonalty.

All Men know how averse they are from the approving of *Christian* Rites and Ceremonies; and, yet, let me tell you, that, whereas the *Greek* Priests do use, at Spring-time, a certain way of Consecration to open the Sea for Sailors (before which time, they will hardly commit their Vessels to the Waters) the *Turks* also observe the same Ceremony: For, when their Vessels are ready to sail, they repair to the *Grecians*, and ask them, whether they have consecrated the Sea? If they say *No*, they desist; if *Yea*, then they set sail and away. 'Twas also a Custom of the *Greeks* not to open the Pits, in the Isle of *Lemnos*, for the digging out of the Earth, called, *Agosphragod*, before the Feast of the Transfiguration of our Lord, *viz. August* 6. The *Turks* also observe the same Custom; and, whereas the *Grecian* Priests did anciently celebrate the Liturgy at that time, the *Turks* will have them do so still; and they themselves stand at a distance, as Spectators only: And, if you ask them, why they do this? Their Answer is, that there are useful Customs practised of old, the Causes whereof are not known. The Ancients, they say, saw and knew more than we; and, therefore, we will not violate their Customs, lest we do it to our loss. This Opinion hath so far prevailed against many of them, that I know some, who in private will baptize their Children, alledging, there is some good in that Rite, and that it was not instituted, at first, without just Cause.

Having acquainted you thus far with the *Turkish* Exercises, let me add one more. They have a Custom derived from the *Parthians*, that they counterfeit flying away on Horseback, and presently turn back and kill their unwary Pursuers. The way they learn to do it, is this: They erect a high

Pole, almost in plain Ground, with a brass Globe on the top of it; about this they spur their Horses, and having got a little beyond, the Horse still galloping, they presently turn about, and flying along, shoot an Arrow into that Globe. The frequent Use hereof makes them expect, that their Bow being turn'd in their Flight, their unwary Enemy is shot through.

'T is time now, you'll say, that I return to my Lodging, lest my Keeper should be angry with me. Well, then; what time is left me from beholding these Exercises, I bestow entirely on my Books, or in Conferences with my Friends the Citizens of *Pera*, originally *Genoese*, or others; yet not without the leave of my *Chiauxes*. These Fellows are not always in the same Humour; they have their lucid Intervals, in which they are more tractable than at other times. When 'tis fair Weather with them, the *Ragustæans*, the *Florentines*, the *Venetians*, and sometimes the *Greeks*, with other Nations, come to visit me, on one Account or another; sometimes, also, I converse with Men of more remote Countries, that come hither, whose Conversation much delights me.

A few Months ago, there came hither a Merchant from *Dantzick*, who had the sole vending of Amber. He wondred to what Use the *Turks* could put so great a Quantity of it, as they bought; or, whither they sent it: At last he was told, that they sent it into *Persia*, where that kind of Juice, or Bitumen, is highly esteemed; for they adorn Parlors, Studies, and Temples with it. He bestowed upon me, a wooden Vessel full of that Liquor, they call *Juppenbier*. It was most excellent Stuff: But I laughed heartily at my Guests, both *Greeks* and *Italians*, who, not being accustomed to this Liquor, could not tell what to call it. At length, because I told them 'twas good to preserve Health, they thought it was some medicinal Drug, and called it a *Syrup*; but they sipp'd and syrupp'd it about so long, that, at one Dinner, they emptied my Barrel.

T HIS Liberty my *Chiauxes* (who now and then are changed) do sometimes give me. They are not only willing I should go abroad, but often invite me so to do: But I, as I told you before, always refuse them, that so they may not think they can do me either good or hurt; and the Pretence I make use of is this, that I have tarried so long at Home, that now I am grown to the Walls of the House, so that if I go forth, it would fall. I will not, therefore, stir abroad, say I, till I go for good and all into my own Country.

As for my Family, I am glad that they go abroad sometimes, for thereby they learn to bear the long Absence from their own Country, the better.

But yet when they make use of this Liberty, the drunken *Turks* often meet and quarrel with them in the Streets, especially, if no *Janizaries* be with them; and, though there be, yet sometimes Blows happen on both sides: And, therefore, it is troublesome to me, to excuse my Domesticks, when they are clamour'd against; yet, I confess, the surliness and vigilance of my *Chiauxes*, in keeping fast my Doors, do in a great Measure ease me of that troublesome Office. Let me give you a late Instance of this kind.

There came lately to me a Messenger from my Master, the Emperor, one *Philip Baldus*, an *Italian*. He was 66 Years old; and, riding faster than his Age could bear, he fell into a Fever. My Physician prescribed him a Clyster, and the same being brought by the Apothecary, my *Chiaux* would not let him in, nor suffer the Medicine to be brought to the sick Man. Inhumanely enough, you'll say; especially, as that *Chiaux* had carried it courteously to me for a long time; but now he was so inraged on a sudden, that 'twas intolerable, for he threatned to cudgel every body that came to me. After he had thus affronted me, I thought of a way to let him know, how little I valued all his bug-bear Threats; which was thus. I set one of my Servants to stand within my Gate, and to bar it; charging him, to open to none, but at my Command. The *Chiaux* comes in the Morning to unlock the Gate, as his Custom was; but his Key availed not, for 'twas bolted. On the in-side he spied my Man, through the Chinks, and calls out to him to open it. Not I, says he; hereupon the *Chiaux* began to be angry, to curse and call Names. Prate while you will, says my Servant, neither thy self nor any of thine shall come in here: For why should I open to thee, more than thou to us? Thou keepest us shut in, and we'll keep thee shut out; do thou shut the Door without, and to be sure I'll shut it within. What, says he, did your Master command you so to do? Yes, said I: However, says the *Chiaux*, let me come in and put my Horse in the Stable: No Stabling for your Horse here, said he. Let me then have some Hay and Provender out for him: Not a bit, says he; go and buy it in the Neighbourhood, there's enough to be sold. I used frequently to make the *Chiaux* sit down at Meat with me, or else send him something from my Table; But now the Case was altered; he stood, fasting as he was, at my Door, his Horse being tied to a *Plane-Tree*, over against it.

THE *Bashaws*, and other Grandees, as they passed by that Place in their return from Court, and knew, by its Trappings, that it was the *Chiaux*'s Horse, eating his Hay under the *Plane-Tree*, they demanded the Reason, why he was not shut up in a Stable, as heretofore? He readily told them all the Matter; that as he shut us up, so he and his Horse were shut out, so that the one could not get Food, or the other Provender. When the rest of the *Bashaws* heard this Story, they laugh'd heartily, and from that Time held it fruitless to think of terrifying me with such frivolous Vexations as the shutting my Doors.

BUT a while after that *Chiaux* was removed, and then we had more Liberty. *Rustan* himself was satisfied how vain his Menaces were by this Story, I shall now relate.

THERE came a certain aged *Sancto*, of great Esteem among them for his Piety, to pay his Court to him; and, among other Discourses, he asked *Rustan* why, since the *Sultan*'s Children were at Discord one with another, which was likely to occasion great Troubles in their Empire, he did not make Peace with the *German* Emperor, that *Solyman* might be secure from Danger on that side? I desire nothing more, says *Rustan*; but how can I bring it about? His Demands I cannot yield to, and my Demands he will not accept, nor can I compel him so to do. I have tried all Ways to bring him to my Terms; I have kept him in the nature of a Prisoner these many Years, I have dealt coarsely enough with him; and yet, alas! he is but hardened the more thereby. When I would shut him up as a close Prisoner in his own House, then he bars his Door on the Inside, that no body can come at him; thus all my Labour is in vain. If another Man had been so hardly dealt with, to avoid the Durance, he would have turned to our Religion; as for him, he cares not a Rush.

THIS was *Rustan*'s Discourse, as some present thereat informed me.

THE reason of their surly Carriage, is this: The *Turks* are very suspicious, that the Agents of Christian Princes have a great Latitude in their Commissions; so that they have Power to alter them, as occasion serves; if they cannot at first get favourable, then they may except of harder Terms. To get out of them the full of their Commissions, they vex their Persons, shut them up close, threaten War, and abuse them all manner of ways.

Some think, that a certain *Venetian* Resident did much encourage the *Turks* to these Courses; for when the Dispute was between the *Venetian* and *Turk*, about *Napoli di Romania*, their Agent had a Charge to try all other ways of Accommodation, without surrendering the City; but if no milder Terms would do, then he had Liberty to part with that City, rather than to engage in a War with the Port: Some *Venetian* Traytor declared this part of his Commission to the *Turks*, unknown to the Resident himself; who rather denied that he had any other Commands, than what he had then proposed, which were the gentlest Terms. The *Bashaws* judging themselves to be deluded, were very angry, and bid him have a care what he said; their Master was not to be mock'd; they knew well enough that he had other Commands, and thereupon, they recited to him the full of his Commission; so that now, said they, if you do not tell us, we shall look on you as a Liar and an Impostor, and then he would be punished as such; and his Commonwealth would certainly be ruined, if the implacable Anger of *Solyman* did once, on this Occasion, stir him up to War against him; and, therefore, speak now, or for ever hereafter hold your Peace: Our Master will not use Entreaties; he hath not Power enough, God be thanked, to command Obedience.

The *Venetian* Agent was so surprized at this Discourse, which he did not so much as dream of, that he very frankly told them all; for which, however, he was very much blamed in his own Country.

Ever since that time, the *Turks* have indulged their Suspicions, that the Christian Agents deal but partially with them; and, therefore, they must humble them to get out all the Truth. Upon this they imprisoned *Velduvic*, the Emperor *Charles*'s Ambassador, 18 Months, and my Collegues more than three Years, and at last sent them away, without doing any thing. As for my self, I know not how long I shall be kept in this Durance; for my part, I see no end of it.

When *Baldus*, that ancient Man of whom I spake before, came to me, they suspected that he had brought me new Commands, which allowed me to yield to harder Conditions of Peace; and they feared that I would conceal them, because I knew well enough their intestine Discords; so that, by dealing harshly with me, they thought to extort the whole Truth from me. Upon the same Design, *Rustan* once sent a large Gourd, called by the *Germans Wasser-plutzer*. They ripen to a delicious Sweetness at

Constantinople; their Seeds are red within, and they came originally from *Rhodes*. By this Present, sent to me by my Secretary, *Rustan* did jestingly insinuate the fear of a War; it was brought me when the Weather was very hot, and the Juice is good to cool inward Heat. He sent this Compliment with it, that I should make use of the Fruit suitable to the hot Season, for it is an excellent Cooler; but I should know, withal, that a great number of those Plants did grow about *Buda* and *Belgrade*, of a much larger size than that which he sent me, meaning thereby *Cannon-Balls*. I returned Thanks for my Present, and told him, I should make use of it; but, for *Buda* and *Belgrade*, 'twas no great wonder they grew there, since there was Plenty of them, even of a larger size, at *Vienna*. It was a pleasure to me, to let *Rustan* know by my Answer, that I could retort Quibble for Quibble.

But to return to the Affairs of *Bajazet*, which you desired to be further informed in.

You may remember that his Father dismissed him some Years ago, upon this Condition, That he should never hereafter affront his Brother, nor raise new Tumults in the Empire, but live quietly and peaceably, as a Brother ought to do. He should remember his Promise made to himself, and not vex him in his old Age; if he did, woe be to him! These Threats had weight with *Bajazet*, as long as his Mother lived; he kept his Word, rather to retain her good Will and Indulgence towards him, than as having any Consideration either for his Brother's Love or Father's good Will. However, quiet he was, for his Mother's sake: But two Years after her Death, looking upon himself as desperate, he cut the Cords of all filial Obedience, and began to resume his former Designs against his Brother, and to execute his Animosity with great spight: Sometimes he laid Ambushes for his Life; at other times he attempted it by open force, and now and then he sent Parties of Men into his Brother's Province, (their Provinces being contiguous one to the other) and if he could catch any of his Domesticks, he used them ill for their Master's sake; in fine, he left no Stone unturned, to lessen his Brother's Credit, finding he was not able to reach his Life.

Besides, he had several Partisans at *Constantinople*, who endeavoured to draw over the *Grand Seignior*'s Guard to his side; and he did not doubt but, as his Design ripened, to come privately to *Constantinople*, and there to abscond among his Friends, till he could have a fair opportunity to make his appearance in public. *Solyman* was soon let into all his Designs, particularly by Letters from his Son *Selimus*, who warned him to take care of his Life; and that, if he did not look upon these Villainous Attempts of *Bajazet*, as pointed at himself, he was much mistaken: For he cared not what he did either against God or Man, provided he might gain the Kingdom. Your Life, Sir, said he, is aimed at as well as mine, and he would wound you through my sides. His Design was contrived long ago, but now he only seeks an opportunity to execute it; and, therefore, pray prevent his Wickedness before you are circumvented by him too late to find any Help: As for myself, I can easily bear all his Injuries; but the greatness of your Danger doth more nearly concern me.

These Informations from *Selimus* did more and more incense *Solyman* against *Bajazet*; so that he put him in mind of his Duty, by Letter, telling him what great Clemency he had used towards him, and what Promises he had reciprocally made to him. Call to mind, said he, those Ancient things, 'tis not so easie for you to get a new Pardon. Leave off wronging your Brother, and creating trouble to me. I have but a little time to live; when I am gone, God will shew which of you shall Reign; in the mean time, don't you disturb the public Peace, nor the Tranquillity of my grey Hairs.

But these Expostulations wrought little upon *Bajazet*, who was fully determin'd to do his utmost, rather than to yield his Neck tamely to his Brother's Sword; for he saw plainly, that would be his Fate, if ever *Selimus* mounted the Throne. However, he answered his Father's Letters submissively enough; but his Words and his Deeds did not agree, neither did he drop the prosecution of his intended Design.

When *Solyman* saw this, he resolved to try another Course, and to remove his two Sons to a greater Distance one from the other; and, therefore, he commands each of them, on a prefix'd Day, to leave his Province (*Chiuta* was *Bajazet*'s, and *Magnetia Selimus*'s) *Bajazet* to go to *Amasia*, and *Selimus* to *Iconium*. This was done, not out of any disfavour to *Selimus*, but only to please *Bajazet*, lest he should break out into Extremes, when he was removed from his Government, and not his Brother from his. Withal, he laid his Commands on them, that, the more they were severed by distance of Place, the more they should be united by Concord of Mind. For (said he) Vicinity of Habitation doth often breed Discord betwixt Brethren, and Servants on both sides do ill Offices to enrage and exasperate the Minds of their Masters, one against the other; and, therefore, obey my

Commands: Him that refuses, I shall count a rebellious Son. *Selimus* immediately left his Province, as being confident of his Father's Favour; but *Bajazet* made many Hesitations, and when he was gone a little way he stopt his Journey, complaining that the unlucky Province of *Amasia* was allotted, as a bad Omen to him; because his Brother was slain there. I should rather, said he, go to any other Province besides, than where the miserable End of my Relations will constantly come to my Mind, and wound my very Soul; and, therefore he desired his Father to suffer him to winter at least where he was, or else in his Brother's Province: But *Solyman* would grant neither of those Requests. By this Time, *Selimus* was marched with an Army which was augmented with some Forces from his Father *Solyman*, (for they were both afraid of *Bajazet*'s Plots) against his Brother, who yet made many Halts and Delays; when, on a sudden, he fetch'd a compass about, and appeared with his Army on the Rear of his Brother, going towards *Prusias*, a City of *Bithynia* over against *Constantinople* on the *Asiatic* Shore; his Father gave consent to his March, as not well pleased with the Delays of *Bajazet*. For they thought thus with themselves, that, if *Bajazet* could win over the Guards to himself, and march to *Prusias*, or even to *Constantinople* itself, their Matters, as to *Solyman* and *Selimus*, would be in great hazard; and, therefore, out of a common fear, 'twas thought most adviseable for *Selimus* to stay there, where he might expect most Aid, in case of Necessity, from the Nearness of the capital Cities. For *Selimus* had not yet Forces enough to encounter his Brother in open Field, with any hopes of Success.

When *Bajazet* saw his Brother's Army in his Rear, and that he got nothing by his Delay, but the certain Knowledge, that *Selimus* should Reign if his Father died, as his Fear added to his Sickness gave some Likelihood thereof; hereupon, he wrote Letters to his Father, wherein he laid grievous Things to the Charge of his Brother *Selimus*, as, that his present March did plainly declare, what a wicked Intent he had towards his Father, who was come so near the *Metropolis*, that he might treacherously compass the Empire, and that he might have but a short Passage over, if his Father died. But, if his Father's Life should balk his desire, then he would suborn some Parricide or other to take it away; and yet, this is the Son, forsooth, said he, that you have in your Bosom; as if he were a very Nonsuch for filial Obedience; whereas I, who never entertained a bad Thought against you in all my Life, but was always observant of your very Becks, am rejected and call out of Favour; and yet the Sum of my Demands is only this, that an unlucky Province may not be designed for my Government; either that which my Brother left, or any other more fortunate one than that of *Amasia*; and, says he, I shall expect an Answer in the Place where I now abide, lest, if my Suit be granted, I be forced to march a great way back; but if your Ears be deaf to my Request, then I will march to what Province you shall command me.

AND the truth is, *Bajazet* had reason to be averse from *Amasia*; for 'tis a Custom among them to build much on Auguries and ill Omens, even in the smallest Matters.

BUT these Letters were otherwise understood by *Solyman*, who was well acquainted with his Son's Fears, and knew that he affected a Government not so remote, but nearer to *Constantinople*, that thereby he might have the better opportunity for Innovations.

THUS *Bajazet* made one Excuse after another for his Delay, and seemed to retard his Father's Pleasure; he listed Soldiers, increased his Army, rais'd Money, and provided all things necessary for his own Defence, and the Conquest of his Brother. *Solyman* looked upon his Design as against himself, yet the crafty old Man dissembled it what he could; for he was unwilling to make *Bajazet* quite desperate. He was now grieved that the Eyes of all Nations were fix'd on that Dissention between his Sons, and therefore he design'd to use some Delay, that the Matter, if possible, might be composed with as little Noise as possible. He answered *Bajazet*'s Letters mildly, telling him, that, as for the Change of Provinces, he was fully resolved to be obey'd therein; and, therefore, he and his Brother would do well immediately to repair to their respective Armies.

As for other Concerns, he need not take care of them, for he himself would so order Matters, that neither his Brother nor he should have any Cause to complain. *Solyman* chose *Pertau*, the Fourth Vizier *Bashaw*, to carry those Letters to *Bajazet*; and, that he might seem to deal impartially between them both, he sent *Mehemet*, the third Vizier *Bashaw*, to *Selimus*. He also laid a Charge on both those *Bashaws*, not to stir a step from either of his Sons, till they had both entred on their respective Governments. This was wisely done by *Solyman* to leave such faithful Moniters with his Children, which would daily put them in Mind of their Duties.

ACCORDINGLY, *Selimus* did willingly admit his Father's *Bashaw*; but *Bajazet*, whose Mind was wholly set upon imbroiling the State, could not endure to have one of his Father's Counsellors obtruded upon him, to be a Witness of his Designs, and to be a Tell-tale to his Father. And, therefore, he dismissed the *Bashaw*, who was willing to have staid, having first courteously treated and presented him with Gifts, according to his present Ability; and he did it with this Pretence, that he had none else to represent his Cause impartially to his Father, but only himself; and, if he would do him so good Offices, he promised not to be ungrateful to him. He desir'd him also to tell his Father, that his Commands should always be to him as a Law, but that he was forced to do what he did, for fear of his Brother *Selimus*, whose Injuries and Affronts he could no longer endure. By this Message of *Pertau*, *Solyman* was assured of *Bajazet*'s Design, though, to colour the Matter, and to put a Blind on his Father's Embassy, he pretended he would hasten to *Amasia*. However, *Solyman* was not slow in his Preparations against *Bajazet*, for he commanded the *Beglerbeg* of *Asia*, though sick of the Gout, to assist his Son *Selimus* with a Body of Horse; and he sent also the most faithful of his Guards to accompany *Mehemet Bassa*, (who was also returned from his Embassies) into *Asia* on the same Errand; and he himself pretended he would gird on his Sword and follow them. But, alas! the Guards shew'd themselves very unwilling to the Service; for they abominated the War betwixt Brothers, as an impious Thing. For against whom should they draw their Sword? Was not *Bajazet* Heir of the Crown too? This unnecessary Discussion (said they) may be compass'd without Blood; neither are we to be forc'd to sheath our Swords in one another's Bowels: As for *Bajazet*, he is forced to do what he doth, in a way of Self-preservation.

WHEN these Rumours came to *Solyman*'s Ears, he sent for the *Mufti* (the High-Priest of the *Turks*, from whom, as from an Oracle, they expect Answers to their Doubts) and puts a Case to him in these Terms.

"How ought that Man to be dealt with, who durst disturb the Peace of the Empire, by taking Towns, and raising Men and Money, while he was alive? As also, What he thought of those, who were assistant to him in that Design, and fought under his Ensigns? and, lastly, what was to be done with those who refused to engage against him, but rather justified his Practises?"

The *Mufti*'s Answer was, "That such a Person with all his Followers were worthy of Death; and they that refused to Fight against him were to be abominated, as Prophane, and Deserters of their Religion."

This Answer was divulged among the Commonalty, and by the Chief of the *Chiauxes* was transmitted to *Bajazet*.

A while after there came a *Chiaux* to *Constantinople*, who had been sent by *Solyman* to *Selimus*, but had been intercepted by *Bajazet*; by whom he sent a Message to their Father, to this effect; that he would never fail in expressing his Duty to his Father, and that he never took up Arms against him, but was resolved to be obedient to him in all Things. The Dispute was only between his Brother and himself, who sought his Life, so that he must fall by his Brother's Sword, or his Brother by his. This difference might be decided in his Father's Life; and, therefore, he desired him not to interpose or assist his Brother, but to carry himself in an exact Neutrality; but if (said he) you pass over into *Asia*, (as Report says you will) to assist *Selimus*, don't think I shall be speedily reduced, for I know whither to retreat; and, let me tell you, the first Day you set Foot in *Asia*, I will destroy all by Fire and Sword, and make it as desolate, as *Tamerlane*, or any of our fiercest Enemies, ever did.

When this Message was delivered to *Solyman*, it did much disturb him, especially when Word was brought to him, that the Town of *Axuar*, which *Selimus*, his Son, was *Sanziach* of, was taken by *Bajazet*; who, after he had exacted a great Sum of Money from the Inhabitants, plundered and sack'd it shamefully.

But *Selimus*, when he heard that his Brother march'd towards *Amasia*, and was already come as far as *Ancyra*, being now freed from the Suspicion of Treachery, which he fear'd in his March, hastened towards *Iconium*, where a Garrison was kept for his Arrival.

'Twas none of the least of *Solyman*'s Cares, which distracted his Mind, lest *Bajazet* should seize on *Iconium*, and so march into *Syria*, from whence there is a large Passage into *Egypt*, a Province not fully settled in Subjection to the *Turks*, and somewhat mindful of the ancient Governors of the *Circassians* or *Mamalukes*, longed for a Change. And if *Bajazet* once got thither, he foresaw it would be a very hard Matter to beat him out, should the neighbouring *Arabians* assist him; who, in hopes of Booty, were ready to take any side. And if, with much ado, he could have been driven out of *Egypt*, yet from thence he might easily be wafted over into any of the *Christian* Countries; whereupon *Solyman*, by all means, sought to stop his March thither, because he thought it would be *Bajazet*'s last Shift; and to that end he had written to most of the Governors of lesser *Asia*, to be watchful, ever and to assist *Selimus*, when he called for their Aid. Accordingly *Selimus* formed a Camp before the Walls of *Iconium*: For he thought it best to wait there for the Auxiliaries of his Father, and not to hazard his All on the doubtful Issue of a Battel.

ON the other side, *Bajazet*, knowing what a hazardous Enterprize he had undertaken, was as vigorous to support his Cause. He hired a great body of Horse, called *Chiurts*, perhaps formerly *Gordianes*, Men noted for Valour, in whom he put Confidence.

THEY, as soon as ever they came to this Army, began their Representation of a Battel on Horseback, which had so much of Reality in it, that many of them were slain, but more wounded.

HIS Camp was pitch'd in the plain and open Fields of *Ancyra*, from which City he was supplied with many Necessaries; and at the Castle thereof he placed his Concubines and Children. From those Merchants, that were rich, he borrowed Money, upon Terms of Re-payment with Interest, if God gave him Success. From thence, also, he was furnished with Arms for his Soldiers.

BESIDES his own Family (consisting of very many among the higher sort of *Turks*) and the *Chiurts* before-mentioned, those that were of his Mother's, or his Sister's, or of *Rustan*'s Faction, came in to him; so did very many of *Mustapha*'s and *Achmet*'s Favourites, fierce and skilful Warriors; for they grudging at the undeserved Deaths of their Masters; were resolved to revenge them with the hazard of their Blood: some also came under his Banner out of Commiseration of the depressed Condition of *Bajazet*, as being necessitated to fly to Arms, his last and only Refuge.

A great many favoured *Bajazet*, because he was like his Father; whereas *Selimus* had not one Feature in his Face resembling him. 'Tis true, he was very like his Mother, a Woman hated while she was alive. He was a big-bellied Man, with swoln Cheeks, and his Face of a deep and uncomely Redness; insomuch, that the Soldiers would seemingly say, *He was cramm'd with Barley-Pudding.* Besides, he liv'd a slothful, banquetting, idle Life; neither was he courteous, or of easy Access, nor did he oblige by any act of Generosity. The Reason he gave, was, that he would not offend his Father, by aiming at popular Applause. Thus he became dear to his Father only, but odious to every body else; yea, those Persons did most disdain him, who coveted a munificent and an active Emperor. The same Soldiers that were wont to call *Bajazet*, *Softi* (a sedentary Man, and given up to his Studies) when they saw that he took up Arms, and ventured his All to defend himself and his Children, now extolled him to the Skies, as a Man of extraordinary Valour. Why (said they, reasoning among themselves) should his Father abdicate a Son that is his express Image? Why should he prefer his slothful, pot-bellied Brother, that has nothing of his Father's Disposition in him? As for *Bajazet*'s taking Arms, Necessity forces him to it, and therefore, he is not to be blamed; for did not *Selimus*, his Grandfather, do the same? What great Precedent could there be? For he did not only arm against his Brother, but Necessity also compelled him to hasten his Father's Death; and yet by this Procedure he established the Kingdom to himself and his Posterity. Now, if *Solyman* did rightfully possess that Kingdom, so gotten, why should his Son be denied to take the same Course? Why should that Fact be thought so heinous in him, which was accounted lawful in his Grandfather? And yet the Case is much different (said they); for *Bajazet* did not take up Arms against his Father, but wishes him a long Life; nay, he would not hurt an Hair of his Brother's Head, if he could be sure of his own Life, against him: But 'tis always lawful to resist Force by Force, and, if possible, to prevent one's own certain Ruin. These Discourses caused many to fly to *Bajazet*, and his Army being now of a moderate Size, without delay, he marches towards his Brother, putting his Life, Fortune, and the hope of his Empire, upon the Event of the Battel; for thus, thought he, my Valour (at least) will be commended, if it be not prosperous; I will endeavour if I can, to break my way into *Syria*, and, if I succeed therein, my Business is done.

SELIMUS waited for him under the Walls of *Iconium*, having a vast Army, encreased by Forces sent him from his Father, and well furnished with skilful Commanders; and, besides all other Necessaries, secured with great Ordnance on every side. *Bajazet* was nothing terrified at all those Disadvantages, but as soon as he came in sight of his Brother's Army, he exhorted his Own, though inferior in Number, in this manner.

Now, says he, *the long wished for Hour is come, wherein you may shew your Valour; do you act as Men, and let me alone to reward you. All my Fortune is in your Hands; my Misfortunes have been irksome some time, but now here is an open Campaign, wherein I may change them for the better, and forget all the Miseries of my former Life. If you conquer, you may expect from me Honour, Dignity, and all kinds of Rewards, befitting Men of Valour. One Victory will crown all our Hopes, though never so vast, and that you may get by your superabounding Valour. As for my Brother's Troops before your Eyes, they are a Company of* Buffoons *under a slothful General; you may easily make way through them with your Swords; what Forces he hath with him of my Father's, though they are his in Body, yet they are mine at Heart. 'Tis* Selimus *alone that stands in the way, both of my Vassals, and of your Happiness too, and therefore, let us both revenge our selves on a common Enemy. And for their Multitude, don't fear them; Conquest is got by Valour, not by Number. God Almighty uses to assist the* Best, *not the* Most. *Certainly, if you consider how the savage Enemy thirsts after your Blood, you will preserve yours, by shedding theirs. In fine,* said he, *I will not only speak, but do. Let me be your Pattern. Do you fight but as valiantly for my Safety, as I shall do for your Advancement, and I'll warrant you the Battel is our own.*

Having finished his Oration, he made towards the Enemy with an undaunted Courage, and in the Front of his Army shew'd himself both a brave Soldier and a skilful Commander, so that he was renowned also by his very Enemies. The Battel was bloody, and many fell on both Sides, and Victory seem'd to hover with doubtful Wings; but at last she inclin'd to that side, where was more Force, a juster Cause, and better Counsel. Just in the nick, there arose such a Wind that it carried the smoke of the Ordnance into the very Faces of *Bajazet*'s Army, so that they fought blindfold, as it were; whereupon *Bajazet*, after much Blood-shed on both sides, was forced to sound a Retreat; but he made it with so little Disorder, and so leisurely, that he seemed a Conqueror, rather than to have lost the Day. Neither did *Selimus* move out of his Camp to pursue him, being well contented to see his Enemies turn their Backs.

After this, *Bajazet*, considering he had disobeyed his Father's Commands, by indulging his own Humour, and being cut off from his

March into *Syria*, which he had design'd, resolved to move in good earnest towards *Amasia*.

Solyman had presently a Messenger sent him of this Victory, and immediately he posted over into *Asia*. His *Bashaws* would not let him go before; *But now* (said they) *you must make haste to press upon* Bajazet *in his Misfortune and to prevent his Recruit; for if his secret Favourites should declare for him, they might cut them out further Work. The Report of your Passage over, will both discourage your Son and terrify all his Followers; and, therefore, make haste, lest he serve you as sometime your Father did, who was more formidable after he was conquered than before, so that his very Overthrow at first was the cause of his Victory in the End.* Neither did they thus speak without Cause; for 'tis incredible how much that Fight, though unfortunate, had added to *Bajazet*'s Renown. That he was so hardily valorous, as, with a small handful in comparison, to set upon the well-disciplin'd Army of his Brother, strengthened too with his Father's Forces; that he was not daunted with the disadvantage of the Place, nor the roaring of the great Ordnance, and that he carried himself in the very Battel, not as a raw Officer, but an expert General. 'Tis true, said they, his Success was not answerable, but his Valour was not inferior; and, therefore, let *Selimus* boast never so much of his Victory to his Father, this we are sure of, that, of the two, *Bajazet* deserved to be Conqueror; and that we may attribute his Brother's being so to any thing rather than to his own Valour. These Discourses concerning *Bajazet*, shew'd him to be Popular, and thereupon they double his Father's Grief and Pain, and his Desire to ruin him. Resolved he was, none but *Selimus* should succeed him in the Empire: For, besides that he was his eldest Son, he had been always faithful and obedient to him; but *Bajazet* had been rebellious, and gaped after the Throne in his Lifetime; and he feared him the more, because he was esteem'd a very valiant Prince, and because also he had openly assisted *Selimus* against him.

For these Reasons he pass'd the Sea into *Asia*, but with a Resolution not to stir from the Shore, but to assist his Son *Selimus*'s Affairs, only at a distance. For why, thought he, should I run any Hazard to bring my own Forces nearer, lest my Army, not fully settled in their Obedience, should be tempted to a Revolt.

I my self saw *Solyman* march out of *Constantinople* in the Year 1559, *June 5th*, tho' against the Will of my *Chiaux*. Let me here present you with a Scene of Mirth, and like a Braggadocio-soldier, tell you of two Battels I had at once; for why, I have Leisure enough (unless you count my Cares my Study) and the larger I am in my Scribling, the more time do I borrow from my Troubles. Hear then, what were my Quarrels.

When I was certainly inform'd that the *Sultan* was ready to pass over into *Asia*, and that the Day was fix'd for his Departure, I told my *Chiaux* that I had a mind to see him march out, and therefore he should come betimes in the Morning and open the Doors, for he used to carry the Keys of my Doors home with him at Night; he promised me courteously, he would do so. Then I order'd my *Janizaries* and my Interpreters, to take me an upper Room in the way the Emperor was to pass, convenient for my View: They obeyed my Commands. When the Day was come, I rose before 'twas light, and expected that my *Chiaux* had opened my Doors; but finding them shut, I sent several Messengers to him, to come and let me out, both my *Janizaries* that waited within Doors, and *Druggermen* that waited to come in: This I did, through the Chinks of the Gate, which was very old; but the *Chiaux* still spun Delays, pretending he would come presently. Thus I spent some time, till I heard the noise of the Guns, which the *Janizaries* use to fire, when their Emperor takes Horse; then I began to fret and fume, seeing my self so deluded. My Disappointment and just Indignation did affect the *Janizaries* themselves: they told me, that if my People would thrust hard with them, they without would so press upon the Valves, which were loose and old, that the Bars would fall out. I took their Counsel; the Doors flew open accordingly, and out we went, hastening to the Room I had hired.

My *Chiaux* had a mind to frustrate my Desire, and yet he was no bad Man neither; for having communicated my Request to the *Bashaws*, they were not willing that any Christian should behold their Prince marching with so small Force against his own Son, and therefore, said they to him, do you promise him fair, but be sure to delay him till the *Sultan* is a Shipboard; then you may think of some Excuse or other to bring you off.

When I came to the House where a Room was hired for me, the Door was shut, so that I could no more enter into that, than I could go out of my own; when I knock'd, no body answered. Hereupon the *Janizaries* again told me, that, if I commanded them, they would either break open the Doors, or get in at Window and open them. I told them, they should not break open any thing; but if they would go up to the Windows, they might: they presently did so, and opened the Door. When I went up Stairs, I found the House full of *Jews*, a whole *Synagogue* of them. They looked upon it as a Miracle, that I should enter, when the Doors were shut; but being informed of the Truth, an old grave Matron, in comely Habit, address'd herself, and complained to me, in *Spanish*, of the Violence I had offered to the House; I told her, she had done me wrong, in not keeping her Word, and that I was not a Man to be thus deluded; she seem'd dissatisfied, and the Time would not admit of further Discourse. In short, I was allowed one Window, which on the back side looked out into the Street, and from thence, with a great deal of Pleasure, I saw all the grand Procession.

The *Gulupagi* and *Ulufagi* marched two by two; the *Selchers* one by one, and *Spahi's* (which are the Names of the *Grand Seignior*'s Horse-Guards) distinguished by their Ranks and Troops; they were about 6000, besides a vast number of the Domesticks of the Prime *Vizier*, and of other *Bashaws*. The *Turkish* Horsemen make a gallant Show; the best Breed of Horses is from *Cappadocia* and *Syria*, and the adjacent Countries; he is set out with Silver Trappings, studded with Gold and Jewels. His Rider is clad with a Coat or Vest made of Silk Velvet, or other fine Cloth of Scarlet, Purple or dark blue Colour, intermixed with Gold and Silver. He hath two Cases hanging by his sides, one holds his Bow, the other his Arrows, both of neat *Babylonian* Workmanship; and so is his Buckler which he bears on his Left Arm, and is Proof against Arrows, Clubs, or Swords. In his Right Hand, unless he desire to have it free, he carries a light Spear, for the most part painted with Green. His Scimiter is studded with Jewels, and made of steel, and it hangs down from his Saddle. What need so much Armour, say you? I'll tell you. They use them all; and that dextrously too. You'll reply, how can he use that Spear and the Bow too? What! will he take up his Spear when he hath broken, or thrown away, his Bow? Not so neither; for he keeps his Spear, as long as he can: But, when he hath occasion to use his Bow, the Spear, being light and easily manag'd, he puts between his Saddle and his Thigh; so that the Point of it sticks out backward; and thus he presses it down with his Knee, as long as he pleases. But, if he fights only with the Spear, then he puts up his Bow into his Case, or else with his left Hand places it behind his Shield. It is not however my present Design to acquaint you with the *Turks* Expertness at Arms; they have obtain'd it by long Use and Experience in War. Their Heads are covered with very fine white Cotton-Linnen, in the midst whereof stands up a Tuft made of Purple Silk, plaighted; some of them wear black Feathers a-top.

AFTER the Horse, a large Body of *Janizaries* followed, being Foot, and seldom taking any other Arms than Muskets. The Make and Colour of their Cloaths are almost the same, so that you would judge them all to be the Servants of one Man. They have no ungainly Habit among them, nor any thing rent or torn; their Cloaths will wear out soon enough, they say, without their tearing them; yet, in their Feathers, Crests, and such-like military Ornaments, they are over-curious, or rather proud; especially, the *Veterans* in the Rear, you would think a whole Wood of walking Feathers were in their Fire-stars and Frontals; after them their Officer and Commanders follow on Horseback, distinguished each by his proper Ensign. In the last Place marches their *Aga*, or General. Then succeed the chief Courtiers, amongst whom are the *Bashaws*; then the Foot of their Prince's Life-Guard in a particular Habit, carrying their Bows bent in their Hands, for they are all Archers; next the Prince's Led-Horses, all with curious Trappings. He himself rode on a stately Prancer, looking sour, with his Brows bent, as if he had been angry; behind him came three Youths, one carrying a Flagon of Water, another his Cloak, another his Bow. Then followed some Eunuchs of the Bed-Chamber; and, at last, a Troop of about Two Hundred Horse closed the Procession.

AFTER I had the Satisfaction of viewing all this, my only care was now to appease my Hostess, she that at my entrance spake to me in *Spanish,* for I heard she was very familiar with *Rustan*'s Wife, and therefore I was afraid she would represent things unhandsomely against me; to prevent which, I sent for her, and told her she should have remembered her Bargain, and not have shut her Door against me who had hired a Room; but, though you, said I, don't remember your Promise, I'll perform mine; yea, I will be better than my word: I promis'd you but seven Pistoles, but here's ten for you, that so you may not repent your Admittance of me into your House. When the Woman thus unexpectedly saw her Hand fill'd with Gold, she was presently melted down into a Compliance, and the whole Synagogue of them fell to Compliments and giving me thanks; and the Woman that was Crony to *Rustan*'s Wife, made one in the Consort, for she always, in my Landlady's name, gave me great Thanks. They offered me *Grecian* Wine and a Banquet, which I refused, but with great Acclamations of all the *Jews*, made haste to be gone, that I might manage a new Dispute with my *Chiaux*, for keeping my Doors fasten'd, when I should have come forth.

I found him sitting mournfully in my Porch, where he began a long Complaint, that I ought not to have gone abroad without his Consent, nor have broke open the Door: that I had violated the Law of Nations thereby, and such like stuff. I replied, in short, that, if he had come betimes in the Morning as he promised, he had prevented all this; his breach of Promise had occasioned it, for his Intent was only to deceive me. I demanded also of him, whether he look'd upon me as an Ambassador, or a Prisoner? As an Ambassador, says he. If you think me a Prisoner, said I, then I am not an fit Instrument to make a Peace, for a Prisoner is not his own Man; but if an Ambassador, as you confess, then why am I not a Free-man? Why can't I go abroad when I will? Captives use to be shut up, not Ambassadors: Liberty is granted to such in all Nations; they may claim it as their publick due: He ought to know, that he was not appointed to be my Serjeant, or Keeper, but to assist me, (as he himself used to say) with his good Offices, that so no other Man might do any Injury to me or mine.

Hereupon he turns to the *Janizaries*, and quarrels with them, for giving me Advice, and helping my Servants, to break open the Doors. They said, I had no need of their Advice: I commanded them to open them, and they obeyed; there was no great Difficulty in it, the Doors were old, and flew open presently; there was nothing either lost or broken. Thus the *Chiaux* was forced to hold his Peace, and I never heard any more of the matter.

A while after, I had also leave to pass over the Sea, for the *Turks* judged it conducing to their Affairs, to treat me nobly in their Camp, as the Ambassador of a Prince in Alliance with them; and to that end, I had a handsome Lodging provided for me near their Camp, where I had all the Conveniences imaginable. I lived there three Months, and had the opportunity to view the Camp of the *Turks*, which was extended all over the neighbouring Fields, and to discover some parts of their Discipline: You will not find fault with me, if I acquaint you with something thereof. Know then, that I cloathed myself as *Christians* do in that Country, and with one or two Attendants walked up and down their Camp *incognito*. The first thing I saw, was, the Soldiers of each Body quartered with great Order in their several Ranks, and that with a great deal of Silence, ('tis far otherwise in *Christian* Camps) all hush; not a Quarrel, nor the least Disorder or Noise amongst them in their Jollities. Besides, they are wonderfully cleanly; no Dung-hill or Noisom smell to offend the Eye or Ear; all their Ordure they bury under Ground, or throw it far enough off. When they have occasion to ease Nature, they dig a Pit with a Spade, and there bury their Excrements; so that there is no ill smell at all. Besides, there are no Drinking-matches amongst them, no playing with Cards or Dice, (the Bane of the *Christian* Army!) I only heard one *Hungarian* common Soldier playing a doleful Ditty on a ill-tuned Harp, and his Companions were howling rather than singing to it; it was the last Words of a Fellow-Soldier, who died of his Wounds on the grassy Bank of the *Danow*; he adjured that River, as her Streams were gliding to his own Country, to commend him to his Friends there, and tell them that he died no ignoble, nor unrevenged Death for the glory of their Nation, and encrease of their Religion. His Fellows groaned out, *Thrice happy he! O that our Case were like his!* For you must know, the *Turks* are of opinion, That no Souls go more directly to Heaven, than those of valiant Men, who lost their lives in the Field; and that Virgins do pour out daily Prayers to God for their Safety.

I had a mind to pass through the Shambles, that I might see what Flesh was sold there; I saw only four or five Weathers at most, hung up dress'd; they were the Shambles of the *Janizaries*, who were at least 4000. I wondred so little Flesh could suffice so many; and was answered, They used but little Flesh, but great part of their Diet was brought from *Constantinople*. When I demanded, *What that was*, they shewed me a *Janizary* near at hand, who was lying down, and boiling Turnips, Leeks,

Garlick, Parsnips, and Cucumbers. He seasoned them with Salt and Vinegar, and, Hunger being his best Sauce, eat them as heartily, as if they had been Partridge or Pheasant.

THEIR Drink was that which is common to all Animals, *viz. Water*; by this frugality, they consult the Health of their Bodies, and also the saving of their Money. And the very time wherein they did this, caused me to admire the more; it was their Fast, (or, as we call it, *Lent*) at which time among *Christians*, even in well-govern'd Cities, as well as in Camps, there is nothing but Sporting, Dancing, Singing, Revelling, Drunkenness, and such like Madness; insomuch, that a *Turkish* Envoy coming once, at that time of the Year, reported at his return, That the *Christians* at certain times grew mad and raging, but sprinkling themselves with a sort of Ashes in their Temples, they recovered their Wits again, so that they did not seem the same Men; thereby denoting *Ash-Wednesday*, and its Eve. The *Turks*, hearing this, were struck with a great Amazement, because they have many Medicines amongst them which cause Madness, but very few that procure a speedy recovery from it.

FOR the Days immediately preceding their Fasts, they do not alter their private way of living in their Worshipping; rather on the contrary, they abridge themselves of some of their daily Commons, that they may prepare for their Fasts, lest a sudden Abstinence might be prejudicial to their Healths.

THE time of their Fast is so appointed, that every Year it comes fifteen Days sooner than the former; the reason is, because they fill not the twelve yearly spaces of the Moon: Hence it comes to pass, that their Fast kept in the early Spring, after six Years, happens at the beginning of Summer; for they measure their Fasts by the course of the Moon, and there are none more irksom to them, than those which fall out in the long Summer-days; for, while they Fast, not a bit, nor so much as a drop of Water, goes down (neither dare they so much as wash their Mouths therewith) before the Star appear in the Evening, the longest Day of Abstinence, being hot, and of course dusty, must needs be very tedious, especially to the poorer sort, who live by their Labour: Yet, before Sun-rise (though not after) while yet the Stars shine in the Firmament, it is lawful for them to eat; and therefore they better endure their Winter Fasts. And that they may not be deceived by the darkness of the Weather, their Priests hang out Lights in Paper-Lanthorns from the top of their *Mosque*, (from whence they are wont, by sound of Voice to call them to the Prayers, as we do by Bells): And this shews that their Eating-time is come; whereupon entring presently into their Temples, and worshipping God in their way, they return to Supper.

In the close of their Summer-Falls, I once saw a great many of them go into a Tavern over-against my Lodging, (where Ice from Mount *Olympus* in *Asia* was always to be sold) and there they ask'd for Icy water, which they drank jetting strangely backwards; for the *Turks* count it profane either to Eat, Drink or Piss in a standing posture, unless in case of Necessity; but they do it bending their Bodies, as Women do with us when they make Water. And whereas in the dusk of the Evening I could not well discern the meaning of that Posture, I was told that most of them drank a draught of cold Water, to make way for their Meat, for otherwise it would stick to their Jaws and they could not swallow it; and, besides, this moisture of their Palate did quicken their Appetites.

In their Diet they are not choice, and after their Fasts they may eat any Meat which was lawful for them to do at other Times. If they fall sick, they omit their Fasts, but with this condition, that when they recover they must fast so many Days over, as they neglected before. But when they are near an Enemy, and ready to fight, lest Fasting should weaken their Bodies, they are allowed to eat; and if a blind Superstition restrains some of them, then their Emperor, at Noon, in the sight of his whole Army eats his Dinner, and by his Example they are all encouraged to do the same.

They use Wine at no time of the Year, they count it profane and irreligious so to do; especially, they abhor it on their Fasts; then no Man is so much as to smell to it, much less to taste it.

I often ask'd, why *Mahomet* was so strict, as to forbid his Followers the use of Wine? In answer to my demand, they told me this Story, that *Mahomet* making a Journey to his Friend, at Noon entred into a House where there was a Marriage-Feast, and setting down with the Guests, he observed them to be very merry and jovial, kissing and embracing one another, which was attributed to the chearfulness of their Spirits raised by the Wine; so that he blessed the sacred Juice, as being an Inspirer of much Love amongst Men: But returning to the same House the next Day, he beheld another face of Things; as Gore-blood on the ground, a Hand cut off, an Arm, Foot, and other Limbs dismember'd; and these, he was told, were the effects of the Brawls and Fightings occasioned by the Wine, which made them mad, and destroy one another: Whereupon he changed his Mind, turning his former *Blessing* into a *Curse*, and forbidding it, as an Abomination, to all his Disciples for ever.

For this Reason all was quiet in the Camp, and the greatest Composure imaginable, especially at their Feast-time: So much did Camp-Discipline, and a Strictness received from their Ancestors prevail upon them!

The *Turks* punish all Vice and Wickedness very severely; their Punishments are, loss of their Places, sale of their Goods, basting with Clubs, Death: But Club-basting is most common, from which the *Janizaries* themselves are not free; though they may not, as such, be put to death. Their lighter Offences are chastised by the Club; their more heinous by cashiering or degrading, which they count worse than Death, because commonly they are put to Death afterwards; for being stripp'd of the Ensigns of *Janizaries*, they are banish'd to the farthest Garrison of the Empire, where they live contemptible and inglorious, till, upon any light Occasion, they are put to Death; yet not as *Janizaries*, but as common Soldiers only.

And here let me acquaint you with the Patience of the *Turks* in receiving that Punishment; they'll receive sometimes an hundred Blows on their Legs, their Feet and Buttocks, with wonderful Patience; so that diver's Clubs are broke, and the Executioner cries out, *Give me another!* Yea, sometimes the Chastisement is so severe, that several pieces of torn Flesh must be cut off from the wounded Parts, before any thing can be applied to cure them. Yet for all this, they must go to their Officer, who commanded them to be punish'd; they must kiss his Hand, and give him Thanks; nay, they must also give the Executioner a Reward for beating them. The Club they are beaten with, they count *sacred*, and that it fell down from Heaven, as the *Romans* counted their *Shield* to do; and, as some Relief to their Misery, they count those Parts wounded with the Rod or Club, to be free from any Purgations, and Expiations after this Life.

When I told you, that the *Turk*'s Camps were free from Broils and Tumults, I must except one, which was made by my own Men: The occasion of it was this. Some of my Servants had a mind to ramble out of the Camp, without any *Janizaries* to attend them; only taking some *Italian*

Renegadoes that professed the *Turk's Religion*. Let me tell you, by the way, that these *Italians* are of good use in that Country, especially in redeeming Captives; for they come to their Masters, and pretend they are either their Kinsmen, or their Countrymen, and therefore, out of Compassion to them, they desire to buy them as their Patrons, for a Price agreed, and so they set them free: But if a *Christian* should make the same proffer to them, they would either refuse, or hold him to a far higher Rate.

But to return: Some of my People, as I told you, gadding abroad, they happened to meet some *Janizaries*, who came from Swimming and Washing themselves in the Sea, without the Badges of their Order on their Heads, only some Linnen being very slightly wrapped about them. These *Janizaries* revil'd my People, knowing them to be *Christians*; for that's the way of the *Turks*, to reproach *Christians*; 'tis a Principle of their Religion, and they think thereby to incline us to exchange our Religion for a better, as they count theirs to be. My Folks being thus provoked, return Jeer for Jeer, from Words they came to Blows, the *Italians* assisting my Men. The cause of the Scuffle was, that one of the *Janizaries* lost the Linnen Covering off his Head, which was thrown I know not whither: Hereupon the *Janizaries* hurry away to their General, complaining of their Wrongs and Damage received by my Servants; for they watch'd them, and found them return'd to my House. Their General presently sent for my Interpreter, who was present at the Conflict: He was seiz'd upon sitting at my Door, and they were pulling him away. I beheld it from a Gallery above, and was much concern'd, that any of my Family should be taken forcibly from me without my Consent, to be carried to the *Bastinado*, (for I understood something of the Matter before); and I could not imagine he would be return'd to me without being well beaten, he being one of the *Turk's* Subjects. Whereupon I ran down, and laid hold on him, commanding them to let him go. They quitted him with much ado, but hasted immediately with far more grievous Complaints to their General, who commanded more of their Company to go and seize those *Italians*, who of *Christians* are said to have become *Turks*; yet he charged them to offer no Violence to me, or to the House where I lodged. They came back presently, and with a great Noise and many Threats, demanded those *Italians*; but they, foreseeing what would come to pass, had sailed back to *Constantinople*. Much Clamour there was on both sides; at last my *Chiaux* at that time, who was an old decrepid Man, out of a jeer thrust some Pistoles into their Hands unknown to me, to buy a new Bonnet in the room of that which was lost; and thus the Dispute ended.

I have been the more punctual in relating this Story, because, on this occasion, I understood from *Rustan*'s own Mouth, what Opinion the *Sultan* had of the *Janizaries*: For he, hearing of this Scuffle, sent a Messenger to me, to desire me to cut off all occasion of Dispute with the *Janizaries* as the worst of Men. You know, said he, 'tis a time of War, whereby *they* may be said to reign, rather than the *Sultan*, who himself stands in fear of them. This he spake, as being well acquainted with the Sentiments of *Solyman*, who always suspected some Men of their own to lie in wait against their *Militia*, who would break out when he had no Opportunity to prevent them.

AND the Truth is, though there may be some use of a standing Guard and *Militia*, yet there are also many Inconveniences attending it, of which this is the chief. Their Emperor is very fearful of them, lest, having the Sword in their Hands, they should alter the Government as they pleas'd, of which there had been many Precedents; yet, there are ways also, whereby this may be prevented.

WHILE I was in their Camp, there came *Albertus de Ubiis*, a worthy and learned Person, born I think at *Amsterdam*, as an Envoy from my Master *Cæsar*. He brought with him some Presents for their *Sultan*, as some Goblets gilt with Gold, with a Clock neatly made, and carried like a Tower on an Elephant's Back; as also some Money to be distributed, amongst the *Bashaws*. *Solyman* would have me deliver these Presents in the Camp, that the Amity betwixt Him and my Master might be more publickly known, and so no Danger at all to be feared from the *Christian* Arms.

BUT to return to *Bajazet*, after the Fight at *Iconium*, who retired to his Government of *Amasia*, pretending to live quietly there, if his Father would permit him so to do. For why? He had sown his wild Oats, and for the future seem'd pliable to obey his Father's Will; and for this he employed sundry Persons to carry submissive Letters to his Father, begging his Pardon: Neither did *Solyman* pretend that he was averse to a Reconciliation with his Son, and therefore he admitted his Messengers into his Presence. He read his Letters, and answered them mildly: So that the Report was spread over all the Army, what an Agreement was like to be between Father and Son; what he had done amiss, was to be imputed to the hot Blood of his youthful Age, provided he would shew himself obsequious for the residue of his Life. This *Solyman* did by the Advice of his *Bashaws*; for the cunning old Man would not declare himself, till he had brought *Bajazet* into the Noose of his own Power. He was terribly afraid, lest out of Desperation he should march furiously into *Persia* (his only place of Refuge,) with such furious Expedition, that all his *Sanziacks* should not be able to get before him. To prevent which Mistakes, he sent many Letters to all the Governors upon the Borders, to watch *Bajazet*, and not to suffer him to escape, if he should attempt it.

IN the mean time, he put all those of *Bajazet*'s Party, that he could get into his Hands, to the Rack; and when he had sifted out of them what he could, he put them privately to Death; amongst which were some that *Bajazet* had sent to clear him to his Father.

THE Kingdom of *Persia* at that time contained all the Countries between the *Caspian* Sea, and the Seas of *Persia*, with some part of *Armenia* the Greater, (though *Solyman*, by taking *Babylon*, *Mesopotamia*, and part of *Media*, had abridged their Empire very much) and other distant Countries even to the Empire of the *Homamia Patisach*, as the *Turks* call him, and over that last part of Land *Sagthamas* was King: The Father had been formerly over-thrown by *Selimus* in a great Fight in the field of *Chalderon*; and from that time the *Persian* Affairs began to decline, for *Solyman* a fierce Engineer press'd upon the very Face of them; and *Thamas*, being much inferior to his Father in Courage, made but weak Defence: For he was wholly given up to Sloth and Idleness, and would sit in his Palace amongst a croud of Harlots, amorously pleasing his Humour; and sometimes consulting Magicians concerning future Events: He had little Care of administring public Justice to his People. This Neglect of his opened the Door to all Injustice and Oppression in every part of his Empire: For the Strong oppressed the Weaker, and Innocence could find no Justice or Defence in his Court.

THE *Persians*, however, have so sacred an Opinion of their Prince, that they believe him happy, that can but kiss the Gates of his Palace; and the Water wherein he washes his Hands, they use for the cure of several Diseases. He hath many Children, but the most promising is *Ismael*, like his Grandfather both in Name and Nature; a beautiful Prince, and a capital Enemy to the Race of the *Ottomans*. 'Tis reported that he was brought forth into the World, with his Fist all bloody, whence it was in every body's Mouth, that he would be a warlike Person; and when he was but young he confirmed that Report, by obtaining a great Victory over the *Turks*. But when his Father made Peace with *Solyman*, 'twas agreed betwixt them, that *Ismael* should be sent Prisoner into the Bowels of his Kingdom, that he might be no Obstacle to the intended Agreement: And yet, as ill us'd as he is, after his Father's Death, 'tis thought, he will succeed in the Empire.

But *Solyman* fearing that *Sagthamas*, (or, as we call him, the *Sophi*) would be more mindful of old Grudges, than of the late Peace to which he was in a manner compell'd; and that, if his Son went thither, he should have much ado to get him thence; and perhaps it might occasion a long War between the Empires, did use his utmost endeavour to stop or take him, before he could come thither. The old Man had not forgot that, a few Years before, *Helcas*, *Thamas*'s Brother, had fled to him, and had been supported by him, and it cost his Brother dear to recover him; and therefore he feared that *Thamas* would pay him in his own Coin, and perhaps recover by the Sword all the Countries he had taken from him. The Design of *Solyman* was kept very secret, yet *Bajazet*'s Friends smelt it out, and therefore advised him by no means to trust his Father, but to consult his own Safety, by what way soever he could. And *Bajazet* was persuaded so to do upon a small occasion, as little Matters often give Weight to greater. There was a Soldier of *Bajazet*'s taken in *Solyman*'s Camp, and hang'd up as a Spy, because *Bajazet* had listed him, after his Father had given him strict Charge to list no more Soldiers. This was warning enough to *Bajazet* to pack up and be gone. Now *Solyman* thought himself sure of *Bajazet*; and, to deceive him the more, he caused his Army to begin their March to *Constantinople* the Day after *Easter*. But *Bajazet*, immediately after Prayers upon *Easter-Day*, gave Orders for marching with Bag and Baggage, and began his unfortunate Voyage to *Persia*. He knew well enough that he went to the old Enemy of the *Ottoman* House, but was resolv'd to try the mercy of any body, rather than fall into his Father's Hands. There marched out with him all that were able to bear Arms; none were left behind but weak Persons, Women and Children, that were not able to bear the fatigue of so long a Journey; amongst which was a new-born Child of his own, with his Mother, whose Innocency he thought would protect them from his Father's Cruelty, and therefore he thought it best to leave them to his Clemency, rather than make them Companions of his woeful and miserable Fight; and the truth is,

Solyman, as yet uncertain what would become of the Father, spared the Life of his Infant-Son at present, and sent him to be educated at *Prusia*.

I would have return'd to *Constantinople*, the Day before *Easter*, but had a great mind to see, how the *Turks* did observe that Festival; and I was not sure that ever I should have so fair an Opportunity again. They were to celebrate it in the open Field, before the Emperor's own Tent. I, therefore, ordered my Servants to take a Room in the Tent of a *Turkish* Soldier, that stood on a rising Ground, and look'd down on *Solyman*'s Tent, which was over against it. Thither went I at Sun-rising, where, in an open Plain, I beheld a vast multitude of turbanted Heads silently standing, and taking down the last Words of their Priest. Every Rank was ranged orderly, and standing, that in the open Field they seemed to be a Wall one to another: The most Honourable had their Station next the Emperor's Train, uppermost in the Camp, and their Turbants as white as Snow. Such diversity of Colours did affect me with a great deal of Pleasure, and the rather, because they stood unmoveable, as if they had grown upon the Place; not a Cough hawking to spit, nor any Sound to be heard; no, nor the least moving of the Head to look backward, or about them. At the Name of *Mahomet*, they all, as one Man, bowed their Heads, even to the Knee; but when the Name of God was pronounced, they all fell prostrate on their Faces, and kissed the Ground.

AND the Truth is, the *Turks* are very ceremonious and attentive in the acts of their religious Worship; for, if a Man doth but scratch his Head when he prays, they think his Prayer is lost. For thus say they, if a Man composes his Body so reverently, even when he speaks but to a *Bashaw*, how much more becoming is that Observance towards God, who is infinitely greater than the greatest of Men?

AFTER Prayers, the whole Congregation was discharged, and they ran up and down ranging over the Fields. A while after the Emperor's Dinner is served up, which the *Janizaries* carry away Dish by Dish, and eat it with a great deal of Mirth and Drollery. 'Tis an old allowed Custom for them so to do, on that day, their Emperor being provided of a Dinner elsewhere. When I had beheld their Show, I returned with great Pleasure to *Constantinople*.

THE remainder of my Talk, is, to acquaint you what become of *Bajazet*, and then I shall ease you of the trouble of Reading, and my self of Writing.

He, as I told you, with his invincible Band, march'd out of *Amasia* with such Speed, that his coming prevented the Report thereof; and those *Bashaws*, who designed to observe his Motion, he came upon unawares. He put a notable Cheat upon the *Bashaw* of *Suvas*; for whereas, there were two ways in his Province by which he might march, and the *Bashaw* had beset the chiefest of them; he sent some before him that pretended to be Run-a-ways, to inform him, he was gone the farthest way about; which giving Credit to, he removed his Troops thither to prevent him, and so left *Bajazet* a free Passage.

He put the like Trick upon the *Bashaw* of *Erzerumen*; for, knowing that the Passage through the Province would be very hazardous, he sent some before him with a counterfeit Message, to salute him, and tell him, that his Misfortunes had reduced him to the most miserable Condition, and therefore he desired him that he might rest a day or two in his Province, at least to get his Horses fed, and new shod.

The *Bashaw* granted his Request, whereas, it was not a commiserating his Case, or that he favoured his Side, but, perhaps, that he might amuse him a little till he had got all his Troops together to ensnare him; for they were scattered, as not dreaming he would be so soon upon him. However, *Bajazet* march'd continually on, allowing his Men no rest by day, and very little at Night. The *Bashaw* of *Erzerumen* seeing himself deceived, made haste to join himself with the other *Bashaws* in his Flight.

For, you must know, as soon as *Solyman* heard his Son was gone from *Amasia*, he commanded a great many *Sanziacks* and *Bashaw* to follow, and upon pain of Death, to bring him either alive or dead: But all in vain, for *Bajazet* fled faster than they could pursue. The *Bashaws* aforementioned, paid dear enough for letting him escape; for *Solyman* put him out of his Place, but *Selimus* put him to Death, together with his two Boys, though not before they had been most detestably used. *Selimus* and *Mehemet Bassa*, and the *Beglerbeg* of *Greece*, pursued *Bajazet* at a greater distance. *Solyman* was much troubled when he heard of his Escape, as being well assured, he would make towards *Persia*; and thereupon he was about to gather all his Forces, both Horse and Foot, together, and so march away to declare War against *Persia*: But his wiser Counsellors stopped his March, alledging the hazard he would run amongst an ungrateful Soldiery: And besides, say they, what if *Bajazet* out of his Temerity and Rashness should send a Company about *Pontus* and the *Palus Mæotis,* and so march back to *Constantinople,* in the Emperor's Absence, where he might, by promising Liberty to Captives, and to the *Agiamoglans,* get upon the Throne, now vacant? These Advices restrained *Solyman* from his Intention.

BAJAZET, all along his March, caused Labels to be fixed to the Doors of the Houses, that he would give double Pay to all the Soldiers that would revolt to him; which made *Solyman*'s Soldiers suspected by their Officers, and the rather, because the common Soldiers talked very freely in favour of *Bajazet.* After much ado, *Bajazet* escaped to the River *Araxes,* which is the Bounds betwixt the two Empires of *Turkey* and *Persia*; and after he had pass'd this River, he scarce thought himself secure, but appointed some of his own Soldiers to guard the Banks, that so the pursuing *Sanziacks* might not pass over: They, however, being but few, were easily discomfited before the *Turkish* Commanders pass'd farther into *Persia*; till at last they met with a great Body of *Persian* Horse, whose Commanders demanded of them, why they invaded another Prince's Territories? Their Answer was, they were to fetch the fugitive Son of their own Prince. The *Persians* told 'em, 'twas contrary to the League to come armed into their Dominions; there was Peace betwixt *Sagthamas* and *Solyman,* which they ought not to violate: As for *Bajazet,* their Prince would do what was fitting; in the mean time they should retreat to their own Country. With this Reprimand they direct their March backward. In the mean time Messengers are immediately sent from *Persia* to *Bajazet,* to bid him return, and to know the cause of his coming, and also to spy out what Forces he had brought with him. *Bajazet* answers, that his Brother's Insolency, and his Father's Displeasure, had driven him out of his own Country, and he was come to *Persia,* as the only Refuge for an oppressed Prince; and therefore, in consideration of the uncertainty of future Affairs, he hoped he would afford him Protection, being destitute of all Things. The *Persian* answered, he was not well advised to repair to him who had made a Peace with his Father; by which they were both bound to serve the same Friend and Enemy, and that League he could not violate: Nevertheless, since he was come, he bid him welcome, and promised he would do his utmost to reconcile him to his Father. Thus his first Entertainment in *Persia* was promising enough; nought but Congratulations, Feastings, friendly Entertainments, and Merrymakings, by which subtle Men disguise their Meanings; nay, there was a talk of a Match between *Orchanes, Bajazet*'s Son, and one of the *Sophi*'s Daughters; and they gave him Hopes, that the *Sophi* would never be at quiet, till *Solyman* had bestowed upon him the Government of *Mesopotamia*, or *Babylon*, or *Arzerum*; for there, say they, you may live commodiously without Fear, as being at a great distance, both from your Brother and your Father too; and if either of them should deal hardly with you, you will have a Father-in-law to fly to, who will afford you Sanctuary. Such Discourses were received among the Vulgar, to divert *Bajazet*'s thoughts from the apprehension of present Danger. The *Sophi* sent many Ambassadors to *Solyman* on this Errand; but whether he dealt sincerely with *Bajazet* to reconcile him to his Father, or no, might be a great question, since in the mean time, he contrived all ways to destroy him; for *Sagthamas* was in a mighty Fear, lest he should nourish a Serpent in his Bosom, and that which encreased his Rancour, was, the wicked design of some, who persuaded *Bajazet* to attempt the destroying of *Sagthamas*; for one of *Bajazet*'s Commanders was heard to say, *Why do we not kill this Heretick, and possess his Kingdoms? For, without doubt, he will one day be the Ruin of us all.* These wild Discourses coming to *Sagthamas*'s Ears, put him upon a Project more necessary than plausible; for *Bajazet* had not many Forces, but very warlike ones; and there were many valiant Men among them that were ready to attempt any Invasion, and therefore he had reason to fear. He was conscious, also, that he had added new Kingdoms to his own, as being conquer'd on pretence of Religion; and who would secure such sickly Subjects, who were weary of their present State, and coveted a Change? To these nothing could be more reasonable than the coming of *Bajazet*. As yet, however, he is more in my Power, than I am in his, and therefore it were best to improve the Opportunity, and treat him no longer as a Guest, but as an Enemy to be chained up. To compass which, no Method was more adviseable than to sever him from his Forces, for then he may be more easily trapp'd; by open Force 'tis hard to seize him, his Soldiers being well train'd and disciplin'd, but mine slothful, unaccustomed to Arms, and, besides, at a great Distance one from another. Hereupon *Bajazet* was advised to disband his Army as unnecessary. He could not withstand the Proposal, though Intelligent Men foresaw the Danger and Consequence: But, alas! He that was under another Man's Roof, must now be at their Beck, who maintained him; especially, since it would breed a Suspicion, if he entertained so much as a thought of Perfidiousness in his Host that entertained him. Hereupon his Men were divided, never to see one another again, and quartered where the *Persians* pleased; and, being put here and there, were, very shortly after slain by them, and their Arms, Horses, and all else they had, fell a prey to the superior Numbers of the Destroyers. At the same time *Bajazet* was clapp'd up in Prison, with his Children; and, to encrease the indignity of the Thing, he was haled even from a Feast, to a Dungeon.

THUS have I satisfied your Desire, in acquainting you with what has been hitherto done with *Bajazet*: 'Tis time now to consider what will become of him for the future: Some think he will retreat to *Babylon*, or such-like Province, on the Borders of each Empire, to be *Sanziack* thereof. Others think it a desperate Case, and that there is no hope of his Life, either from *Solyman* or *Sagthamas*; but that he will either be sent back hither to be put to Death, or strangled in Prison there.

FOR the *Persian* weighed every thing in his Thoughts, when he put *Bajazet* in Prison; he knew him to be of an aspiring and courageous Spirit, far superior to his Brother; and that, if he should succeed his Father in the Empire, it might do *Persia* much more Mischief than ever *Selimus* could; for he was but a slothful Prince, and not at all for a War, and therefore some thought he would never escape out of his Hands; for to be sure he can never be a Friend to one he hath injured so much. Some think one thing, and some another: For my part, I think it will be an intricate Business. For, as *Bajazet* is in Troubles, and the Issue undetermin'd, they will not easily make War on *Christendom* at this Juncture. They labour to obtrude on me certain conditions of Peace, having some Letters that will please my Master, but they allow me no Copy of them, as heretofore they used to do; so that I suspect Fraud in the case, and therefore do peremptorily refuse to send those Letters to *Cæsar*, unless I first know their Contents; and if they deceive me by a false Copy, then the Blame lies at their Door, not at mine: By this means I shall free my Master from answering their captious Letters; for I am sure he will accept of no conditions of Peace but such as are honourable. But, you'll say, if you refuse to accept of their conditions of Peace, 'tis one step towards a War. Let that be as it will, I judge it more adviseable to leave all free to the events of future Ages: But the not sending their Letters, if that be a Crime, I shall take up on my self; and I shall easily clear my self, if the Issue of *Bajazet*'s Affairs do not answer their Expectation; since it is yet very difficult, though not impossible, for the

Turks are not irreconcileable to those Ambassadors, who study to do their Master the best Service they can amongst them. And besides, the declining Age of my Prince will be some advantage to me, who the *Bashaws* thinks is fitter for rest and quiet, than for the Fatigues of an unnecessary War. 'Tis true, my Pains will be prolonged hereby, but I shall think them best bestowed, if they succeed at last.

Thus, Sir, I have written you a Book rather than a Letter; and if I have offended you in it, the fault is yours rather than mine: What I did was at your Request, and Readiness to please a Friend, hath always been counted a Vertue in Friendship. Yet I hope these Things will be as pleasant for you to Read, as they were delightful for me to Write; for, let me tell you, as soon as I put Pen to Paper, I love to wander abroad in my Mind, that so I may as it were, deceive my Confinement as long as I can, and converse with you as if we were together. What things seem frivolous and needless, you must take, as proceeding by word of Mouth in familiar Conferences among Friends. Men may be allow'd to tittle tattle in a Letter, as well as in common Discourse. If I were to write Inscriptions for Churches and Temples, to be seen of all Men, Circumspection and Care must be used; but not when I write to you and a few private Friends. I aim not at Fame; if my Lines please you, I have enough. You will say, perhaps, I might have written better Latin: I grant it; but what if it were beyond my Ability? It was not for want of any good will; and yet, let me ask you, what good Latin can come out of uncouth *Greece,* or barbarous *Turkey*? If you have any Value for my Letters, you shall have more of them after my Return to *Vienna,* if ever God permit me to return: If not, excuse the last Trouble I shall give you. Farewell.

Constantinople, June 1st.

www.ingramcontent.com/pod-product-compliance
Lightning Source LLC
Chambersburg PA
CBHW081618100526
44590CB00021B/3500